Devil in the Details

Scenes from an Obsessive Girlhood

"Jennifer Traig is exactly like Ellen DeGeneres. That is, if De-Generes were a frizzy-haired, Old Testament–obsessed, anorexic, Jewish teenage girl with obsessive compulsive disorder. Traig's touching, jocose . . . memoir of her 1980s teen years in California is a wild ride. . . . By treating her family with kid gloves and making jokes at her own expense — so refreshing in the confessional genre — Traig elicits plenty of sympathy for her devils."
— Henry Goldblatt, *Entertainment Weekly*

"Funny, poignant, gorgeously written."
— Christopher Kelly, *Fort Worth Star-Telegram*

"Jennifer Traig imbues her story with humor and wit, and sheds light on a rare condition." — Regis Behe, *Pittsburgh Tribune-Review*

"I have known Jenny Traig for a while, but did not know she was so odd — so dangerously strange. *Devil in the Details* is breezy and entertaining, and will give great pleasure to anyone who is buggy, obsessive, and who therefore should be jailed. The rest of us, who are sane and perfect, read a book like this with detached amusement, glad that this sort of behavior is limited to teenage Jewish girls."
— Dave Eggers

"Traig writes with intellect and humor. . . . A fantastic read."
— Ashley Baker, *YM*

"Devil in the Details is hilarious, frightening, good-natured, and deeply moving all at once, a compulsively readable comic memoir that combines the bizarre best of Roz Chast and Dostoyevsky."
— Mark O'Donnell

"By turns hilarious and harrowing, this spiritual-psychological autobiography poses a classification conundrum: it fits as comfortably alongside David Sedaris (especially *Naked*, with its similarly themed essay 'A Plague of Tics') as it does next to those by Oliver Sacks. . . . Uproariously funny."
— *Booklist*

"Best new book you're not reading."
— *Jewsweek*, Jewriffic Awards

"What makes this wonderfully winning memoir so unusual is that the author has the detached intelligence and wit to keep laughing at herself, without ever forfeiting her human dignity, or descending even for a moment into self-pity. As a writer, Jennifer Traig is consistently good company."
— Phillip Lopate

"It's as if David Sedaris and Anne Lamott got together and let loose a fountain of one-liners about an obscure neurological malfunction."
— Jill Wolfson, *San Jose Mercury News*

"Traig's behavior makes her seem like a character on *Seinfeld* or *Curb Your Enthusiasm*. . . . Readers who can't get enough of wacky childhood stories by Augusten Burroughs, David Sedaris, and Haven Kimmel may like *Devil in the Details*."
— *Publishers Weekly*

"*Devil in the Details* is hilarious and painful at the same time. What makes this book succeed is the emotional authenticity of these revelations about obsessive compulsions. To read it is to be reminded of your own teenaged weirdness and the miracle that you're not even crazier than you are."
— Katharine Weber

Devil

in the

Details

Devil
in the
Details

Scenes from an Obsessive Girlhood

Jennifer Traig

BACK BAY BOOKS

Little, Brown and Company
New York Boston London

Back Bay Books / Little, Brown and Company
Hachette Book Group USA
237 Park Avenue , New York, NY 10017
Visit our Web site at www.HachetteBookGroupUSA.com

Originally published in hardcover by Little, Brown and Company,
September 2004
First Back Bay paperback edition, February 2006

Library of Congress Cataloging-in-Publication Data
Traig, Jennifer.
    Devil in the details : scenes from an obsessive girlhood / Jennifer
Traig. — 1st ed.
        p. cm.
    ISBN 0-316-15877-1(hc) / 0-316-01074-X (pb)
    1. Traig, Jennifer.   2. Obsessive-compulsive disorder in
adolescence — Patients — Biography.   3. Obsessive-compulsive
disorder — Religious aspects — Judaism.   I. Title.
RJ506.O25T736 2004
362.196'85227'0092 — dc22
                                                          2004001417

10 9 8 7 6 5 4 3
Q-FF
Text design by Meryl Sussman Levavi
Illustrations by Peter Bernard
Printed in the United States of America

For my family, Alain, Judith, and Vicky,
who have the patience of saints

Contents

TODAY I AM A MANIC 101

IDLE HANDS 118

SUNRISE, SUNSET: THE HOLIDAYS 131

ALL IS VANITY 154

ORANGE GIRL 170

SACRE BLEU 188

HELL ON WHEELS 208

SHALOM BAYIT 223

Devil
in the
Details

Scruples

MY FATHER AND I were in the laundry room and we were having a crisis. It was the strangest thing, but I couldn't stop crying. And there were a few other weird things: I was wearing a yarmulke and a nightgown, for one, and then there were my hands, red and raw and wrapped in plastic baggies. My lip was split. There were paper towels under my feet. And weirdest of all, everything I owned seemed to be in the washing machine, whites and colors, clothes and shoes, barrettes and backpacks, all jumbled together. Huh.

"Huh," my father said, examining the Reebok Esprit Hello Kitty stew churning through permanent press. "You want to tell me what happened here?"

Wasn't it obvious? The fumes from the bacon my sister had microwaved for dessert had tainted everything I owned, so now it all had to be washed. But this sort of rational explanation hadn't been going over well with my father lately. I scrambled to think of another, turning lies over in my mouth: it was homework, an experiment; it was performance art, a high-concept piece protesting the consumerization of tweens. I glanced up at my father and down at the machine, then dragged my baggied wrist under my nose and exhaled. "I don't know."

We didn't know. Many years later we would learn that what happened was a strange condition called scrupulosity, a hyper-religious form of obsessive-compulsive disorder. It hit me when I was twelve and plagued me, off and on, throughout my teens, making every day a surprising and mortifying adventure. The disease manifested itself in different ways, but they were always, always embarrassing. Sometimes I had to drop to my knees and pray in the middle of student council meetings, and sometimes I had to hide under the bleachers and chant psalms. Sometimes I couldn't touch anything and sometimes I had to pat something repeatedly. Sometimes I had to wash my hands and sometimes I had to wash someone else's. Sometimes I had to purify my binders. Sometimes I had to put all my things in the washing machine.

Scrupulosity is also known as scruples, a name I much prefer. Scruples sounds like it could be a pesky, harmless condition: "I ate some bad clams last night, and today I've got the scruples." Scruples is cute and saucy. "Oh, you and your scruples," I imagined my date saying, laughing at the coy way I examined my lunch for spiritual contaminants. Scruples also evokes the fabulous Judith Krantz novel that would lead me to expect a far different disorder, one in which my mental illness compelled me to fulfill the fantasies of Beverly Hills debauchees — for a price.

But it's none of that. In fact, *scruple* is the Latin word for a small sharp stone. Originally this denoted a measure; the idea was that the sufferer was constantly weighing the scales of her conscience. I imagine a pebble in a shoe, perhaps because I was hobbled by constant nagging worries and by the undersized pointed flats I wore to punish myself. They pinched and chafed and matched nothing I owned, but weren't nearly as uncomfortable as the doubts that plagued me every second of every day.

Scrupulosity is sometimes called the doubting disease, because it forces you to question everything. Anything you do or say or wear or hear or eat or think, you examine in excruciatingly minute detail. Will I go to hell if I watch HBO? Is it sacrilegious to shop wholesale? What is the biblical position on organic produce? One question leads directly to the next, like beads on a rosary, each doubt a pearl to rub and worry. Foundation garments, beverages, reading material: for the scrupulous, no matter is too mundane for a dissertation-length theological interrogation. Oh, we have fun.

But it was 1982, and we didn't know any of this then. We didn't know what this was or where it had come from. It had come out of nowhere. Well, there were things. There was the fact that I'd been having obsessive-compulsive impulses since preschool. These had been stray and occasional, and while my parents may have thought it was strange that I couldn't stop rearranging the coasters, they didn't think it was anything worth treating. The compulsions had grown with me, however, and now they loomed like hulking, moody preteens. There was also the fact that I'd been systematically starving myself for a year and was no longer capable of making any kind of rational decision. I sometimes wore knickers and pumps, wore fedoras and a vinyl bomber jacket to *seventh grade,* setting myself up for the kind of ridicule that takes years of therapy and precisely calibrated medications to undo. No, I was in no condition to make rational decisions, no condition at all.

And into this mire had come halachah, Jewish law. I had begun studying for my bat mitzvah, twelve years old and a little bit scattered and crazy, and suddenly here were all these wonderful rules. They were fantastic, prescribing one's every movement, giving structure to the erratic compulsions that had begun to beat a baffling but irresistible tattoo on my nervous system. Halachah and latent OCD make a wonderful cocktail, and I was intoxicated. Suddenly I wasn't just washing; I was purifying myself of sin. I wasn't just patting things; I was laying on hands. Now my rituals were exactly that: rituals.

And my gosh, it was fun. The endless chanting, the incessant immersing of vessels — I couldn't get enough. The obsessive behavior quickly evolved from a casual hobby to an all-consuming addiction, a full-time occupation. It happened so fast. One day I was riding bikes to McDonald's like a normal kid; the next, I was painting the lintels with marinade to ward off the Angel of Death.

I don't remember what came first, but I think it was the food. At this point I'd been having problems with food in an obsessive but secular way for about a year. I had begun eliminating foods from my diet, first sugar and shortening, and then cooked foods, then food that had been touched by human hands, then processed foods, and then unprocessed. By January we were down to little more than dried fruit, and my nails were the texture of string cheese.

But then came these lovely laws to give shape to my dietary idiosyncrasies. It was so sudden and unexpected, this revulsion to pork and shellfish, to meat with dairy. I hadn't asked for it, but here it was. Suddenly I was keeping kosher. I was sort of keeping kosher. I was afraid to tell my parents, so I was hiding it, spitting ham into napkins, carefully dissecting cheese from burger, pepperoni from pizza.

"Is there a reason you're hiding that pork chop under your plate?" my mother wanted to know.

"Oh, I'm just tenderizing it," I lied, thwacking it with the Fiestaware.

"Is there something wrong with the shrimp?" my father inquired.

"Seafood recall, they said on the news. You all can play food poisoning roulette if you like, but I'm giving mine to the cat."

The food could have kept me busy forever, but I was ambitious. One by one, things fell away. I would wake up and know: today, no television, it's blasphemous. Then: no more reading *Seventeen*, it's immodest, it's forbidden. A partial list of things I considered off-limits: exfoliation, hair color, mix tapes, lip gloss. Oh, I had so much energy, and there were so many laws I could take on, and when I ran out I would just make up my own.

The fact that I had no idea what I was doing held me back not at all. Despite six years of Hebrew school and a bat mitzvah crash course, I knew next to nothing about daily Jewish practice. I'd retained a couple folk songs and some Hebrew swear words, but that was about it. The only source texts I had were a King James Bible, an encyclopedia, and the collected works of Chaim Potok and Herman Wouk in paperback.

But this was enough. The Bible alone was chock-full of minute instructions, obscure decrees banning the plucking of this and the poking of that. It was these small, specific directives I favored. I was less interested in big guidelines like commandments than in the marginalia of Jewish practice, the fine print, the novelty laws and weird statutes. Had my impulses been secular, I would have observed the funny forgotten ordinances on the law books banning the chewing of gum by false-mustache wearers or the dressing up of one's mule.

As it was I zeroed in on the biblical laws governing agriculture and livestock. Later, as I grew older and more disturbed, I would focus on the laws concerning contamination by death and bodily fluids, but for now it was plants and pets. We did not have any crops, but we had a lawn, and that was close enough. I contrived to leave the corners unmown so the poor could come and glean. I imagined hordes of kerchiefed, unwashed peasants descending to gather sheaves of crabgrass at dawn. "Oh, thank you, Jennifer the Righteous!" they would cry, their dirty faces shining with happiness, blades of grass caught in their blackened teeth.

They never showed up, but I was undeterred. The Bible said, and I did. As for livestock, we had only a dog and a cat, but I was determined to care for them as my faith intended. Halachah instructs us to feed our animals before we feed ourselves. It's a good law, designed to teach compassion, but it wasn't specific enough for me. Were you supposed to feed them just once, before breakfast, or did you have to feed them every time you wanted to eat? I decided to err on the side of zeal and fed them before every meal, every snack, every glass of water. The dog was active enough to burn off the extra calories, but the cat quickly ballooned to twenty pounds. My mother flinched every time I approached the can opener.

"Oh, I swear, you're not giving the cat any more food, are you? She stepped on my foot this morning and I think she broke a toe."

Goodness knows I wanted to stop. The cat's stomach was brushing the linoleum; I knew I wasn't doing her any favors. And I *dreaded* feeding her. Opening and serving her meaty wet food was a lengthy and excruciating process that involved washing my hands and the utensils multiple times. If any cat food splattered, the cleanup could take twice as long, and if the spray landed near my mouth — invariably it would, as I spastically flung the food into the bowl — all hell broke loose. I would be compelled to wash my mouth in cold water, then hot, then cold again. After my lips were split and bleeding I would give up and decide the cat food had rendered me fleishig, as though I had actually eaten the meat; to avoid mixing the meat with milk, I wouldn't touch milk for the next six hours.

That was fine; I had no time for ice cream when there were so many other laws to observe and question. There was this one: the Torah commands a master to pay for his animals' misdeeds. Our dog had been committing misdeeds all over the neighbors' lawns for years. Was I now compelled to offer restitution? Exactly what form should that take?

This probably wasn't a concern in normal Jewish homes, I realized, even observant ones, but I couldn't help myself. I didn't know any better. I knew nothing. I did not know, for instance, that girls weren't required to wear yarmulkes. I agonized over the issue. Should I wear a yarmulke all the time, even to school? I really thought I should, but I just wasn't brave enough. A fedora, yes; but a yarmulke was too much.

After several weeks of debate I decided I really only needed to cover my head when I prayed. The thing was, I couldn't stop praying. Since I rarely had a hat with me, I grabbed whatever was near: napkins, paper towels, Kleenex. Mostly I just used my hand. My fingers kept flying up to hover over my head while I quickly muttered a self-composed blessing. I pretended I was waving, or swatting, or scratching. This was not as effective a ruse as I imagined, and I ended up looking not only crazy but infested.

My head was certainly buzzing. It was a beehive, a switchboard with a hundred extensions lighting up at once. The only thing that quieted my brain was prayer. I wished it were something else. Prayer was dull and time-consuming. If only I found relief in more entertaining activities, like watching television or styling hair.

Instead, I had prayer. Soon my day was dominated by lengthy devotional sessions, conducted every morning, afternoon, and evening. I knew Jews were supposed to pray three times a day, but I didn't know the actual prayers, so I composed my own. First was ten minutes of chanting for a dozen missing children whose names I'd memorized after seeing them on the news. Next was extended pleading on behalf of all Americans held hostage abroad. After that I apologized for everything I had done wrong or would do wrong. Then I prayed for my family, begging forgiveness for their excessive pork consumption, and finished up by praying I wouldn't die alone.

On Saturday the prayers were doubled and tripled. Because there wasn't a synagogue service within walking distance, I conducted my own. Because I did not know what a service consisted of, I made one up. From nine o'clock until half past noon I sat primly in my room, reading my Bible and my *Junior Jewish Encyclopedia*, line by line, not moving to a new line until I was sure I'd understood the last one completely. When that portion of the service was concluded, I read the "Torah Thoughts" feature in the Jewish newspaper, followed by the wedding announcements. Then I got on my knees and did back exercises. I was fairly certain this wasn't part of the traditional Shabbat service, but I thought it was a nice closer. Sound body equals sound mind and sound spirit.

Sabbath observance had come as an afterthought. I was already observing the minutiae of jubilee year agricultural laws; I figured I probably should be keeping Shabbat, too, whatever that entailed. I had only the slimmest grasp of what was and wasn't permitted. The Torah forbids spinning, threshing, and sowing, and though I had some new hobbies, they didn't include these activities. My questions were far more practical. Was it okay to go to the bathroom? Was it okay to *wipe*? This wasn't the sort of thing you could ask your rabbi.

To be on the safe side, I decided, I would do as little as possible. Was reading magazines okay? Better not. Climbing stairs? Oh, why ask for trouble? Activity after activity fell away. When there was nothing left I decided it wasn't enough to just observe Shabbat; I needed to observe it retroactively. I was horrified that I hadn't kept the Sabbath day holy up until now. According to the Torah the penalty for forgetting the Sabbath day was death. By age twelve, I figured, I'd violated it about ten thousand times, and now it was time to make things right. I would go through everything I owned, determine what had been purchased or made or washed on a Saturday, and get rid of it.

This process was made much easier thanks to an earlier compulsion. For the previous two years I'd had a mandatory bedtime ritual — I had to type one line describing something I'd done that day, in all caps, punctuated by twelve exclamation points. This document now proved incredibly useful, because if I'd "WATCHED BEST EVER EPISODE OF MANIMAL TONIGHT!!!!!!!!!!!!" — Friday night — I could figure that the entry that came next — "GOT AWESOME LACOSTE SHIRT AT MARSHALL'S TODAY!!!!!!!!!!!!" — was from Saturday and that the shirt was now tainted, ill-gotten, and had to go.

This amounted to a mammoth pile of stuff. I couldn't keep it with the rest of my things, as the Shabbat-violating profanity of it all was contagious and could infect everything. It had to be quarantined, banished. For years I'd been using the cupboard under my bathroom sink as a graveyard for failed experiments, moldering jars of homemade bubble bath and Frankensteinian combinations of soap, and this seemed as good a place as any to hide it all. I turned the cupboard into a musty Gehenna of hair ribbons, socks, stationery supplies, and clothes.

But I quickly outgrew it. There was so much to hide. Before long I'd established lots of little burial sites, hiding spots, dumping grounds, where I could excrete my unwanted things and kick sand over them.

I could not throw these things away. There was an urge to quarantine, but there was an equally strong urge to hoard, save, store away. Newspapers were the worst. It's a classic OCD compulsion, so widespread and primal I often wonder what obsessive-compulsives hoarded before the invention of the printing press. Did they fill their homes with parchment? Were stone tablets stacked up to their ceilings? Did their families beg them to throw out the scrolls, at least the ones they'd already read?

We're lucky now; newspapers are fairly compact. I was even luckier, because I didn't have to save the whole paper, just little bits of it. I had noticed that some religious people dropped vowels when they wrote certain words, like G—d and L—rd, because these words were sacred and couldn't be thrown away. I had to clip them out, them and all their synonyms. I was left with hundreds of tiny scraps, hundreds of *Holy Fathers* and *Blessed Kings*. When I couldn't figure out what to do with them I started tucking them into books, hiding them in the pages of the dictionary and the encyclopedia. Every time someone looked up a word a shower of holy confetti would fall out. "Wonder how those got there," I would murmur, hoping no one saw me as I gathered up the scraps and kissed them to erase the insult of being on the ground.

It was around this time that my family began to notice I was acting funny. I'd managed to hide it for the first few months. The haphazard kashrut and lengthy prayer sessions had passed unremarked. But the hand gestures, paper hats, and floor kissing had become impossible to ignore. The washing, too, had become a problem. Given the amount of pork we kept in the house it was a safe assumption that every surface was liberally basted with pig fat. I felt compelled to wash my hands upwards of fifty times a day. Getting clean enough to eat was an elaborate and time-consuming process I had to begin a good half hour before dinner. The meal was invariably delayed, but if I touched anything I would have to start all over again, so I wandered around the house with my hands held up in front of myself like a surgeon until it was time to sit down.

"All scrubbed in for your big casserolectomy, Dr. Traig?" my mother asked.

"Just doing some isometric hand exercises here," I lied. "Every girl wants shapely wrists and well-toned fingers."

But the gloves, it seemed, were off. My family had politely ignored my behavior for the first few months, but now they were relentless. They began confronting me, and I began lying.

"Is there a reason your napkin is full of meatballs?" my mother wanted to know.

"Can you tell me why there's an altar of pinecones in the backyard?"

"Would you know anything about the bleach spots on the upholstery?"

I lied more than I ever had in my life. I lied, and lied and lied. Sure, not lying was one of the Ten Commandments, and not eating meatballs wasn't even in the top two hundred, but lying seemed preferable.

I had to lie. My new habits were secret. I was open and honest about my other neuroses, my hypochondria and my fear that the dog could read my thoughts, but I knew this new business was something that had to stay hidden. This was impossibly weird. This wasn't a kooky affectation, like, oh, vegetarianism. This was something they locked you up for.

Unlike Jewish law, getting locked up was something I knew about. By age twelve I'd spent more time on a psych ward than is probably healthy for a preteen. Three years earlier, my favorite babysitter had started acting strangely, doing odd little things like refusing to eat and passing out and threatening to hurt herself, and now she was hospitalized fairly regularly. The hospital was only a block from our house, and I was permitted to visit her, on the locked ward, whenever she was there.

This may not have been the healthiest environment for a grade-schooler. But I liked it. As far as I was concerned it was a magic forest of secondhand smoke and Thorazine, quiet and peaceful, where I could pass a happy hour watching soap operas in the lounge with the other patients. The meds made them glazed and sluggish, but they were all very nice.

"You want a cigarette, sweetheart?" they offered. "You want some of this hard candy? Listen to me, I'm going to tell you something very important, because you're a nice little girl. Jesus is coming, and when he does, the aliens are going to start eating people, but don't worry, I'll tell them to just leave you alone."

I'd spent so much time there, had shared their snacks and magazines. Maybe I'd caught something. Maybe I was just like them. Or maybe, and this was even scarier, maybe I was perfectly sane. Maybe the troubling thoughts weren't coming from my own malfunctioning brain but from heaven. Maybe I was a prophet, sent to teach the people of earth to wash their hands properly. Maybe that was what was coming next. Maybe tomorrow I would wake up and feel compelled to wear a sandwich board and hand out leaflets, to yell crazy exhortations through a bullhorn.

"Sons of Adam, use the hand soap, the liquid kind! The bar stuff just makes you dirtier!"

"Daughters of Eve, use a paper towel to turn off the faucet!

Otherwise you'll just pick up the dirty germs you were trying to wash off in the first place!"

It was too horrible to contemplate. In the meantime I would just keep wearing paper towels and lying. I figured I'd go on living the rest of my life this way, maybe find a job sterilizing headsets and eventually settle down with someone who found my affectations charming.

But my family kept asking questions, and finally, after months of washing, it was time to come clean. There followed a series of many teary scenes in which I confessed to everything. The stash of first fruits, the disposable yarmulkes, the urge to lick the parquet flooring — I accounted for it all. But the explanations I offered, now true, were no less crazy than the lies I'd been telling the past few months. My family was bewildered.

"Let me get this straight," my father puzzled. "You're telling me you're acting this way because *the Torah commands you to?* That's the reason? Are you sure you're not sniffing paint? You sure you're not just drunk?" My parents knew how to deal with grain alcohol. But what were they to do with grain offerings?

Still, they tried. They read some articles, asked some questions. They tried to learn the lingo my new lifestyle would require, words like *parve, milchig,* and *treyf.* My mother mastered these in no time but continued to insist on calling Shabbat the Sabbath, which I didn't like at all. It sounded so Puritan, so seventeenth-century, and I worried that next she'd be calling me Goody Traig.

As it was, she liked to pretend I was Howard Hughes. "Those toenails are coming in nicely, How," she trilled. "Soon they'll be long enough to clack against the linoleum and we'll be able to hear you coming. Now stay right there, I'm going to go clean the canned fruit with Handi Wipes and fix you a snack."

I didn't care for the flip tone, but if that was the trade-off, that was fine. If the price of getting to act crazy was having my family think I actually was crazy, that was okay, so long as I didn't have to stop washing furniture and binding sheaves. It was so liberating, not having to hide and lie and pretend any longer. My family continued to badger and restrict me, but now I could argue with them openly. It was almost fun, almost funny.

"Why won't you wear the new dress we bought for you?" my father wanted to know.

"Because it is written: Thou shalt not garb thyself in robes of hybrid fibers."

"I think mayhap thou hast misunderstood," my father returned. "Now rise up, return to thy quarters, and garb thyself as thine elders commandest thee, or thou will lose thy Bible-reading privileges."

Still, they let a lot of things go. It wasn't so much that they approved, or even accepted it, but they were amused. I was wearing paper hats and talking to the bookcases. It was sad and annoying, but it was also fairly entertaining, and we didn't have cable. I had become the Jenny Show, a kooky sitcom, wacky high jinks twenty-four hours a day. Sure, I mostly aired repeats, but I was the only thing on.

But it was always the same rerun, and things quickly got out of hand. It's a short journey from giving up bacon to deciding you shouldn't bite your nails because the protein that composes them might have come from pork. The washing became incessant, the prayers never-ending. Things seemed okay for a month or two.

Then suddenly we were in the laundry room and all my belongings were floating in detergent. Suddenly we were having a crisis.

I imagine there were conferences, hushed discussions between my parents, consultations with psychologist friends, calls to relatives. What were they to do with me? There was no precedent. They couldn't discipline me by taking away the things I loved; I'd already taken them away myself. Grounding me was pointless. And I actually liked being sent to my room.

In the end my parents came up with a plan as pragmatic and no-nonsense as they are: they drew up a contract. The terms were clear and simple. I was permitted to wash my hands after bathroom visits and at no other time. I could pray up to an hour a day, but not if I was going to do the weird head-patting thing. I could keep Shabbat, but I would not be allowed to ruin the day for everyone else. I could not proselytize. I could not supervise my mother's cooking. I could not rewash clean dishes, clothes, or body parts. Furthermore, to reverse the damage I'd done with overzealous scouring, I was now required to use emollients. I may have been the only twelve-year-old girl in the world who was contractually obligated to moisturize and deep condition and wear Lip Smackers.

If I failed to do any of these things, the contract stipulated that all my friends would be informed of my idiosyncrasies. The mouth-scrubbing, the altar-building, the praise-dancing — they would learn about it all and would be encouraged to share it with whomever they liked. My sister requested that an amendment be added providing that she be the one to inform them all, and my parents granted it as a reward for being so patient with me all these months.

I don't know why this worked. The only thing my parents were threatening was embarrassment, and I'd been embarrassing myself daily for close to a year. Maybe I'd just had enough, or maybe I knew that as much as I could torture myself, my classmates were capable of much worse. Would they ridicule me with a Carrie-style dousing in 409? I didn't want to find out.

And so I stopped. I'm sure there must have been months and months of tapering and adjustment, but I don't recall any of it. I don't remember getting better or struggling with impulses. There was no counseling and no drugs. This time, this first time, I just stopped. I still prayed, still avoided pork and stayed in on Saturdays, but the allure of scrutinizing ingredients and purifying vessels was gone. Over the next six years, the scrupulosity would beckon again and again, shiny and exciting, and I would submit to the inevitable relapses. But this time I just stopped.

In Judaism someone who becomes religious is called a *baal tshuva* — a master of repentance, or, literally, a master of returning, of circling back. I liked the name because it seemed so apt. I circled. I was a master of circling, a pacer, a ruminator, caught in my neural loops. For the next few years, I would circle back to scrupulosity, then back to sanity, then back and forth again. Eventually I ended up sane but religious, baal tshuva in the ordinary sense.

The continuation of my religious practice was a huge disappointment to my family, who'd greeted my initial interest in Judaism with a withering caveat: "You can pray all you want, but we're not going to stop eating pork." They are the family that bacon built — friends sometimes call us the Traifs — and they could never comprehend my rejection of their staple food and lifestyle. They had raised me to express my Jewishness by renting Woody Allen movies, not by keeping kosher and observing Shabbat.

When I was at my sickest, they painted a dark picture of what my future as an observant Jew would entail: "You will marry a man who wears knickers and a fur hat, and when you are out in public passersby will laugh at you. He will make you shave your head and wear a wig so unattractive that people will think it was assembled from squirrel hides. The only restaurants you'll patronize will be cheerless establishments where you will be insulted by rude Israeli waiters and forced to pay exorbitant prices for gray, leathery brisket. Because all your time will be spent in synagogue, you will never, ever have a tan. You will wear frumpy skirts, socks with sandals, and you'll never enjoy corn dogs, shellfish, or drinkable wine." How crushed they were when I got better only to keep up this ridiculous religious practice. They had hoped I would come to my senses and join the rest of them at the clambake.

I never did, but things turned out okay anyway. They were wrong about the fur hats and the bad food. The tan, however — they nailed that one on the head.

A GUIDE TO PROPER HAND-WASHING TECHNIQUE

Did you know that your hands are loaded with bacteria and other contaminants? They're filthy! They spread disease! Oh, it's just awful. And it's not scientifically possible to sterilize your hands. You can, however, get them really, really clean. Here's how!

1. First, you need to get some water going. We want it hot, hot, hot! The hot-water tap is contaminated, but that's okay, because you're about to wash. Touch it again, just to show how brave you are. Touch it one more time. Three taps wards off bad things. Now we're ready to wash!

2. Next, choose your poison. What kind of soap is for you? Bar soap is out; other people have probably used it (a possibility too horrible to contemplate), and even if it's unopened it's made from animal fats, which is revolting. The whole thing just seems so dirty. Liquid soap it is! Choose an antibacterial formula if you're worried about contamination from germs. If you're worried about contamination from death, choose dishwashing liquid. It's so death-free it's safe to use on plates and flatware! But only if it's BRAND-NEW. Even then, you never know. Okay, let's skip the soap altogether. Plain water will be fine.

3. Rub your hands together vigorously and scrub, scrub, scrub. The Centers for Disease Control recommend you wash your hands for ten seconds, but what do they know? If they're such geniuses why do people still get hepatitis? A full minute,

minimum. How about this: you keep your hands under that tap until you answer the philosophical question "Is water clean?"

4. I don't know if water is clean. What if water isn't clean? What if water just makes you dirtier?

5. You'll wash and wash and wash but you'll never be safe.

6. Okay, try not to think about it. Let's just say water is clean and move on.

7. But what if it's not clean?

8. We're moving on. This next part is tricky. Your hands are clean — but they're wet. How to get them dry without getting them dirty again? The air-dry technique is best. Sure, it's slow, but it's safe. Simply hold your hands in the air until they're completely dry. Be sure not to touch anything! If you touch something, or if for some reason you think you maybe touched something, go back to Step 1. Yes, let's go back to Step 1 just to be safe.

9. Now we're in a hurry. You're going to have to dry your hands with paper napkins. That's fine. Just make sure it's a new package. Did you touch the part of the package that was sealed with glue? Is that glue? Glue is dirty. Wash again, just to be safe, then dry your hands on a napkin that absolutely for sure didn't touch the glue.

10. Use a napkin to turn off the tap and another napkin to open the door on the way out. Some people won't even touch the door with a napkin; they'll just wait until somebody comes to open the door for them. But they're crazy!

Devil in the Details:
A Primer

EVERY MENTAL ILLNESS has its pros and cons, but for all-around appeal, you can't beat OCD. It's not as colorful as multiple personality disorder or as exhilarating as bipolarity, but for consistent amusement, it's your best bet. It's not a bad one, as mental illnesses go. Obsessive-compulsives make great party guests. With our droll little quirks, we provide plenty of conversation material, and we're sure to help clean up afterward. In fact, we'll probably start washing the glassware halfway through the first round and may return three hours after the party has ended to bleach down the floors. Except for the tedium, the time commitment, and the incessant badgering, we're a riot.

We are legion, an army of millions. Though most of us will go to any length to hide our compulsions, we recognize one another. The guy using a paper towel to turn the restroom doorknob, the child counting his eyelashes, the old man wearing Kleenex boxes for shoes — these are my brothers. We are a secret tribe. We're like Freemasons, except that our secret handshake is followed by a vigorous washing session.

The mystery is how one becomes a member. No one knows precisely what causes the disease. In the past it was blamed variously on demon possession, bad parenting, fluid retention and — my favorite — constipation. The theory, I suppose, is that your head might clear once you've crapped your brains out. The invention of psychoanalysis brought an end to the stake burnings and enemas but did not lend the disorder any new dignity. Freud held that sufferers were stunted in the anal-sadistic phase. Nice.

This was the prevailing theory when my OCD first surfaced. I was three; I probably *was* stuck in the anal-sadistic phase. But I didn't know anything about that, or care. I was too busy satisfying the compulsive urges that sprang out of my nervous system and commanded me to do things like poke the tomato plant with a stick and sit on the baby. These activities didn't seem to arouse much concern from my parents. Soft and plump and cosseted in double knit, my sister could easily be mistaken for a beanbag. As for the tomato plant, it probably deserved a good poking. "That's right, honey, you show that plant who's boss," my mother encouraged. "Say, sweetheart, is that your sister under your backside? If you're going to sit on her face, just make sure that either her nose or mouth is clear. Okay?"

These compulsions seemed to pass for normal. My compulsion to swat furniture, less so. This was impossible to ignore or explain. It drove everyone crazy, but I couldn't stop. Twenty or thirty times during the course of a meal, I would hop out of my seat, spin around, smack the bookshelf behind my chair, then spin back. It was not an activity I particularly enjoyed. While I was spanking the furniture, my cereal was getting soggy, my sister was eating my bacon, and my parents were expanding my vocabulary with a series of increasingly profane threats. "Sweet mother of crap, Jennifer. What did the bookcase ever do to you? If you're going to smack anything, smack your sister. She's the one who's eating all your bacon."

A good idea, but it was like scratching your left leg when your right one itches; only the bookcase would do. Next came threats. "You jump up one more time and you'll be taking the rest of the meal with your hands taped to that damn bookcase," my parents warned. "We'll give you a straw and you can drink your Cheerios." I scowled, sulked, spun around some more. Didn't they know this wasn't any fun for me, either? Didn't they understand I didn't want to do these things? Couldn't they see?

Maybe it's best they didn't. Had I been diagnosed, I could have been treated with high colonics and Valium, things that, though fun, are really wasted on a child. OCD was just so poorly understood at the time. It's only in the last fifteen years that there's been a shift toward biology. Now we know OCD is a brain disorder, related to Tourette's syndrome, that originates in the basal ganglia, the gray clump of cells in the center of the brain. I imagine them as a rat-shaped cluster, its tail tickling my nervous system. The analogy seems fitting given the rodentlike characteristics of the disorder. OCD sufferers are like hamsters on treadmills, all industrious activity with nothing to show for it. If we were compelled to turn windmills or crank generators rather than alphabetize the canned goods, we could solve the energy crisis.

Instead our major contribution to society is that, like rodents, we are pests. No surprise that Freud named his famous obsessive-compulsive subject the Rat Man. Unlike the Rat Man, I was never plagued by obsessions of rats biting my backside (anal sadism, indeed), but I did, in a sense, have rats on my mind. When my OCD was flaring, it truly felt like a rodent had burrowed its way into my brain, my basal ganglia like a scrabbling animal, each movement of its tiny claws compelling me to do things against my will. A flick here made me inspect the juice glasses; a flick there, and I was sterilizing all the flatware.

Basal ganglia injuries can bring the condition on almost instantly. The rest of us have to work at it. It's a thousand tiny impulses, building on one another. First you decide it's a good idea to check the oatmeal bin for bugs. Next you're going through all the canisters, and before you know it, you're wearing a hazmat suit and examining the frosted flakes for ground-up glass. Each action further enforces the obsessive-compulsive circuit. When the disease is full-blown, sufferers are firmly entrenched in neural loops that make them repeat thoughts and actions over and over. In other words, your brain keeps getting back in line for the same carnival ride it didn't enjoy in the first place. You lose your sunglasses, you throw up on your shirt, and two minutes later you're back on the Whizzer. Wheeeee.

In spite of all this, obsessive-compulsives aren't delusional. OCD is not a psychosis. Sufferers never lose touch with reality. Sure, we do crazy things, but we *know* they're crazy. We don't want to do them at all, but we can't help ourselves. I've done plenty of things that truly *were* deluded — dyeing my hair magenta, working at a summer camp, using a home tooth-bleaching kit — but the difference is that I thought these were good ideas at the time. I never thought it was a good idea to disinfect my binders, but I had to do it anyway. Back on the Whizzer we go.

The ride is the same; so is the scenery. There can be no greater proof of the uniformity of human hard wiring than the sameness of obsessive-compulsives' triggers. Cross-culturally and trans-historically, we zero in on the exact same things: details and doorknobs, electrical sockets, locks, light switches, blood, bugs, and germs. AIDS is a recent favorite; with its overtones of sex, blood, and contagion, it seems custom-made for the obsessive-compulsive imagination. Surely these fears are evidence of some evolutionary remnant, an instinct for self-preservation gone haywire, but I can't help wishing our cathexes were more colorful. Why couldn't we be obsessed with, say, tropical drinks or fad dances? It would be much more entertaining if the disorder compelled us to mix banana daiquiris or perform the lambada.

Perhaps our obsessions are entertaining enough. In real life we are meek and law-abiding, but in our minds we are murderous sex fiends. Most obsessive-compulsives fear they are going to stab a loved one. Many of us can't bear to be around knives at all. This fear isn't all that irrational; knives are dangerous, and goodness knows even loved ones can push it. Our other fears, however, make less sense. Though we are neither pedophiles nor animal-lovers, we fear that we are going to rape the baby and the housecat. We worry that we are going to make passes at friends, family members, strangers we find repulsive. Straight obsessive-compulsives often fear that they are actually gay. We all worry that we are unwittingly peppering our speech with profanities. We replay conversations over and over in our heads, convinced that we blurted out something unforgivable. When I was a young child this wasn't too bad, but by adolescence it was a real problem. After a perfectly pleasant exchange with a great-aunt I could spend hours trying to recall whether or not I'd told her to go screw herself the hard way. I would beg my sister, Vicky, for reassurance. "You heard our conversation. Did anal sex come up at all? I know it sounds crazy, but I think Aunt Rose may have raised the issue."

"No, you were the one who brought it up," Vicky would respond, sick to death of talking me down. "You told her you were going to give it to her all night long. I wouldn't expect a birthday check from her this year."

Cruel, sure, but I could hardly blame her. Reassurance-seeking is the obsessive-compulsive's most annoying habit, as incessant as it is disturbing. We tend to ask loved ones things like, "I'm not going to poison you, am I? I'm really worried I'm going to poison you."

But our loved ones needn't worry. Though obsessive-compulsives' primary fear is that we might hurt others, we're much less likely than the general population to actually do so. OCD is a closed circuit. Obsessive-compulsives are the original navel-gazers, too caught up in our own worries and routines to unleash our negative impulses on others. Even if we were inclined to do harm, we wouldn't have time. Compulsions tend to keep us busy around the clock.

Here, too, there's little variance. We all love to write lists. We like to clean. We enjoy worrying. And then we have our specialties. There are the washers, the checkers, the counters, the tappers. Most people fall into more than one category, but one behavior tends to dominate. A hopeless dilettante, I dabbled in a few. Tapping captivated me for a while, then washing, then checking. Each was a variation on a theme, a spell chanted in another language.

What I wanted, simply, was magic. I'd grown up with Samantha, Sabrina, and Jeannie, those sparkling blondes whose tics and twitches could solve any problem. My OCD just seemed like more of the same. These jerky urges, I was sure, gave me powers. There is a magic in OCD, revolving as it does around lucky numbers, magic words, formulas, and rituals. Tapping the bookcase meant everything would be okay. Washing the plate three times meant my family wouldn't die. So I tapped the bookcase, I washed the plate, and guess what: everything was okay. They didn't die. Abracadabra. Magic.

But the props, the props were lame. Instead of top hats and rabbits I had furniture and flatware, plants and plates. They didn't get any better as I grew older. By the time I was seven, most of my compulsions revolved around stuffed animals. Stupid stuffed animals. I hated them. They were so babyish, birthday gifts I'd gotten instead of the more adult playthings I really wanted, like checkbooks and carpet sweepers. The animals were just so *needy,* so much work. They had to be washed and dressed and cared for. Worst of all was the compulsory feeding, conducted every night after I'd been put to bed. They ate air served up in a plastic panty hose egg. Each animal got five servings, consisting of fifteen bites each. The feeding was strictly ordered, with the animals lined up by size. I moved down the line with my egg, making eye contact with each while maintaining a breathless narrative chatter. "Biteforyoubiteforyoubiteforyoubiteforyou

biteforyou," I exhaled. "Now, abiteforyoubiteforyoubiteforyou biteforyou." I had twenty or thirty stuffed animals, and if they skipped dessert I could be done in forty-five minutes. My mother finally noticed what was going on and confiscated my plastic egg, with an admonishment to cut the crap.

That was fine. I had other hobbies. I'd become a voracious reader, which prompted a whole new genre of compulsive behavior. For the better part of second grade I couldn't stop internally narrating everything that happened to me. I put my conversations in mental quotes, my actions in descriptive passages, pausing in cross-eyed concentration as I tried to get it all down in my head. "Stop looking at me like that," my sister would threaten ("'Stop looking at me like that,' her sister threatened"), and I would raise a questioning eyebrow to buy time ("She cocked an eyebrow inquisitively"). That would just make my sister angrier ("'I mean it, stop it,' she repeated. 'STOP IT. STOP IT!!!'"). The narrative always finished unhappily ("The oafish beast twisted her sibling's delicate arm, then grabbed her dainty palm and spat in it. 'That'll teach you to stare at me,' the harpy warned"). The end.

Learning to read was probably the worst thing that ever happened to me. It just gave me so much material, the newspaper most of all. "Dear Abby" and "Ask Beth" probably weren't the best reading material for a seven-year-old, but they were the only features in the local paper that held my interest. Advice columns opened my eyes to everything that could go wrong. Their readers' problems became my own, giving me things to obsess about while I sat awake not feeding my stuffed animals. What if my boyfriend pressured me for heavy petting? What if I discovered my best friend's husband was having an affair? What if my in-laws refused to cut their son's apron strings?

All sad stories, but the one that kept me up nights was from an unfortunate reader who wanted to know if her prematurely sagging breasts had been caused by jogging without a bra. I already had plenty of reasons to dread PE — boredom, unflattering uniforms, the possibility of exertion — but I didn't know a droopy figure was one of them. This sent me spiraling into a panic. Unable to think about anything else, I finally addressed the issue in a tête-à-tête with my mother. She was not sympathetic. "First of all, you're about six years away from puberty. And since when do you jog? Sitting on the couch watching eight hours of cartoons a day, as you do, is not going to affect your bustline either way. Worry about something that might actually happen, like brain atrophy or butt cramps." Dissatisfied, I stomped off to my room to draft a letter asking for advice on dealing with an insensitive mother.

Advice columns, after all, covered just about everything. But I don't remember anyone writing for help with their obsessive-compulsive impulses. In the late '70s, OCD was not the disease du jour. (TMJ was. Burt Reynolds had it! It was glamorous.) MS, CP, SIDS — they tackled all the other acronyms. But OCD wasn't even really a disease yet. People didn't know they had it.

I certainly didn't. And after a while, I didn't have it anymore. It had moved on. When it came back again, five years later, it would be wearing a yarmulke and a prayer shawl, causing crises in the laundry room. My OCD mutated into scrupulosity, and it got its hooks into me like garden-variety OCD never had.

I liked scrupulosity because it got right to the point. It's the purest form of OCD. In a sense, all OCD is religious, of course;

it's a disease of ceremony and ritual. (Freud, for the record, argued the opposite — that all religion is obsessive. Inflammatory, sure, but if you've been pestered by a doorbell-ringing, *Watchtower*-wielding missionary you won't argue the point.) OCD certainly looks like religious practice: we perform our compulsions with exacting devotion, we repeat incantations, and you know what cleanliness is next to. But with scrupulosity, the rituals truly are rituals, the incantations are prayers. The stakes, moreover, are infinitely higher. With other forms of OCD you fear that if you don't perform your compulsions, your father might get sick; with scrupulosity, you fear you'll cause a global spiritual Armageddon or, at the very least, damn yourself to hell for all eternity.

It's no surprise that scrupulosity is the oldest recognized form of OCD. There's a fine line between piety and wack-ass obsession, and people have been landing on the wrong side for thousands of years. There are records of obsessive-compulsive monks going back to the sixth century. By the twelfth century, scrupulosity had been named, recognized, and even lauded by the Catholic Church. Later, as sufferers wore clergy down with their annoying doubts and worries, it was recognized as a disease requiring psychiatric intervention, but for a long time scrupulosity was seen as a virtue.

And why not? Some of Christianity's best and brightest had it. The Little Flower, Thérèse of Lisieux, suffered excruciating scrupulosity throughout her teens before going on to become the patron saint of Fresno. Ignatius of Loyola was tortured by a flaming case that compelled him to pray seven hours a day. Martin Luther's compulsion to confess was so severe and constant that his confessors threatened to cut him off. John Bunyan's scrupulous obsessions were relieved only by spending hours chanting "I will not, I will not, I will not" while flailing his arms. It's not as exciting a celebrity roster as, say, that of syphilis, but it's enough to staff an all-star benefit on the History Channel. Today the condition is common enough that there's a Scrupulous Anonymous group. I've never joined, so I can't tell you if they subscribe to all twelve steps or if they just repeat one step over and over.

I can tell you that, like most resources for the scrupulous, they are Christian. If obsessive-compulsives are rat men, the scrupulous are church mice. Scrupulosity affects Christians and Jews in nearly equal numbers, but only Christians address the issue with support groups and socials, chat boards and pamphlets. Judaism, so verbose on most other subjects, is nearly mute on this one. We have no vocabulary for it. Still, it seems clear that there's a history of Jewish scrupulosity. The scrupulous Rat Man himself was Jewish, and there are tales of rabbis who compulsively rechecked their locks, who examined every grain of salt for contamination, who could spend three hours picking out the perfect matzo for the seder. True to neurotic form, Jewish tradition argues that these sages had perfectly good reasons for their behavior: their good-for-nothing sons left the doors unlocked, the salt had been contaminated once before, and what's so wrong with wanting to serve nice things?

The problem may be that traditional Jewish observance and compulsive behavior are almost too close to differentiate. Judaism has codified a whole choreography of compulsive, compulsory gestures and tics. We reach up to touch the mezuzah each time we pass a doorway. We kiss the prayer book when we close it, the Torah when we approach it, any religious object when we drop it. We cover our eyes when we say the Shema prayer, and bend, bow, and straighten when we say the Aleinu. The Amidah, the silent prayer, is a ballet of compulsive movement. We take three steps back and three steps forward and bow before we begin; bow twice more; rise up on our tiptoes three times; jump up and bow, then bow left-right-left and take three steps back and three steps forward again. We repeat verses, shout responses at given prompts, sit and stand, sway and nod. With all the swaying, flailing, and outbursts, a Jewish congregation could easily be mistaken for a Tourette's convention.

Orthodox Judaism looks so much like scrupulosity that some psychiatrists, and my father, have asked if they might be one and the same. The psychiatrists, at least, came to the conclusion that they are not. They're close, sure, but there are some vital differences. Orthodox Jews are motivated by spiritual duty and rewarded by a sense of fulfillment; the scrupulous are motivated by circuitry and rewarded by chapped hands. Orthodox Jews may look nuts, but in fact they're perfectly well-adjusted. In other words, pre-tearing toilet paper for the Sabbath may be crazy, but it's not compulsive.

If, however, you happen to be both compulsive and Jewish, you're in for the ride of your life. The Jewish scrupulous experience is extraordinarily rich. Sure, Christians have that snappy "What Would Jesus Do?" catchphrase to govern their ruminations and inspire new ones, but even as a Jew, I find the phrase sacrilegious. (Is one really supposed to characterize Jesus as a best girlfriend? When it is applied, you end up asking questions like,

"What would Jesus do if his boyfriend pressured him for some tongue after cheerleading practice?" It's a bad formula.)

Christians may have the slogans, the support groups, and the brimstone, but Jews have an endless supply of minute laws. They have the devil; we have the details. Scrupulous Christians have only the Bible for crazy source material. Jews have the Talmud, the *Shulchan Aruch,* the Code of Ethics, and a host of other texts, all chock-full of obsessive minutiae legislating matters as esoteric as the cleanliness of hairnets. There are 613 commandments, which is enough to keep even the most industrious compulsive busy all day long. Every movement and moment is regulated, from the morning Modeh Ani prayer to the bedtime Shema. The order in which you put on your shoes, the order in which you tie them, the way in which you wash and dress and eat and speak — all these things are prescribed in exacting detail. Almost every activity requires a blessing before and after. There's even a blessing for using the bathroom, which, considering the binding capacities of traditional Jewish cuisine, is totally understandable.

It's almost too much, an embarrassment of riches for the compulsive practitioner. As a result, most scrupulous Jews tend to overlook, even violate, the bulk of the laws while observing one or two with excruciating care. Compulsions tend to come before commandments. I could violate three or four commandments in one fell swoop. I was happy to lie to my dishonored parents while breaking the Sabbath, as long as it was in the service of getting my hands ritually clean.

The great thing about having so many laws was that you could pick and choose, and move on to the next when the last lost its magic. I tore through scores. When the agricultural laws lost their luster I turned to the laws proscribing the mixing of kinds: meat and milk, linen and wool, oxen and asses, and, in my interpretation, diet and regular. Next came the Levitical regulations regarding bodily fluids. Here I thought I'd truly found my métier, but this, too, grew old, and I moved on to the Temple construction laws. At some point I became absolutely convinced I needed to learn all the rules regarding the ephod, the temple vestment. What if the Messiah came and I needed to sew an ephod? What if I ended up on the Urim and Thumim committee? I had to know the regulations. No one wants to be the jerk who messes up the Messianic Age. No one wants to be the idiot who gets us all kicked out of Eden again.

Because one's immortal soul — Jewish or Christian — is on the line, scrupulosity can be one of the hardest forms of OCD to treat. The therapy and pharmaceuticals that can fix other obsessive-compulsive disorders often aren't enough; clergy has to be brought in, too. Oddly, religion is often what helps the sufferer get over it. There are numerous accounts of terribly afflicted people whose scrupulosity disappeared as soon as they entered a religious order. Well, no surprise. If faith in a higher power can get people to stop doing really, really fun things like cocaine and Keno, it can certainly get them to stop sterilizing can openers.

Faith was almost all I had. At the time, the good drugs and really effective therapeutic protocols hadn't been invented yet. We didn't have anything. We didn't even have a diagnosis. But we had rabbis, and so it was that I ended up in a series of synagogue offices, whimpering while my parents reeled off the list of my most recent peccadilloes.

I had expected the rabbis to be impressed with my piety, to collude with me, to tell my parents they were lucky to have such a devout child. Instead they shook their heads and sighed and gently suggested I spend more time with my friends.

This, of course, was exactly what they were supposed to do. Though Jewish literature doesn't speak of scrupulosity, and these rabbis didn't either, they clearly knew what I had and what to do. They said, we've learned about this. They said we've seen this before. In the end their response was the same as the Church's, the same as the APA's, the same as my mother's: to insist, in as reassuring a tone as possible, that I cut the crap.

A standard sermon joke: A synagogue is plagued with mice. The congregation hires exterminator after exterminator, to no avail. The mice keep coming back. Finally the rabbi has an idea. He stays up all night sewing tiny yarmulkes and prayer shawls. He places some cheese on the bimah, and when the mice come to eat it, he bar mitzvahs them. They are never seen in synagogue again.

The process was more or less the same for me. There was some chanting; some words from the rabbi; several years of behavior modification, relapses, therapy, and pharmaceuticals; and then, like the bar mitzvahed mice, my scrupulosity went away. Poof, like magic.

MUSICAL CHAIRS: A GAME

Everyone loves party games, but the traditional ones are dances with the devil. Piñatas, pin the tail on the donkey — you're just asking for trouble. Why risk an eye-goring, a concussion, or eternal damnation when you can have just as much fun with this engaging activity? It's guaranteed safe and guaranteed fun. Best of all, you can play alone. The prize: your physical and spiritual security!

NUMBER OF PLAYERS: 1

OBJECT: Find someplace to sit! With all the chairs in this house, it should be easy, but . . .

RULES:

1. Players may not sit in the white chair, the comfortable one across from the TV. Sure, white is the color of purity and holiness, and if the chair were still actually white this might repel sin, but sadly, that's not the case. The favorite chair of the pets and the site of their frequent self-administered genital baths, it has become gray, shredded, and contaminated beyond repair. Move on!

2. Players may not sit on either the leather couch or the loveseat. The loveseat is forbidden for the name alone. *Loveseat.* This is just asking for it. The couch isn't much better. First of all, it's leather, and hence steeped in meat and impurity and death.

You *might* be able to sit on it if you hadn't just consumed dairy, but you have, and you've got bigger problems than that, anyway. You're pretty sure the couch was purchased on Shabbat. Finally, your sister and her friends like to sit there, and let's be frank: a couple of them are suspected dischargers. That couch is contaminated, all right. Just forget about it.

3. Players may not sit on the Eames recliner. It is your father's favorite chair and to sit there would be disrespectful. Furthermore, it is leather (see Rule 2).

4. Players may not sit on the tweed couch. True, it rarely gets used and is therefore less likely to be contaminated. But it's a pullout. It's a pullout, a *bed,* and it seems possible that overnight guests may have had sex on it. Keep moving.

5. Players may not sit on any of the beds, because they are beds.

6. Players may not sit on any of the armchairs, because who knows what they're stuffed with.

7. Players may not sit on either the kitchen or dining room chairs. Food gets dropped on the upholstery all the time. To sit on these chairs is to sit on ham.

8. Players may not sit on any of the desk chairs, because they used to be kitchen chairs.

9. Players may not sit on the floor, because this prompts your father to yell, "This isn't Morocco, and in this house we sit on chairs, dammit." To sit on the floor is to disrespect your parents. Furthermore, as your father points out, "If you're worried about impurity, the floor is the last place you should be sitting. As far as the pets are concerned, the floor is just one big shag-pile toilet."

10. Players may not sit on any of the toilets. This goes without saying. Don't think about toilets. Don't think about toilets. Don't think about toilets. Oh, now you're going to have to go wash. Game over.

Half-Breed

I FIRST LEARNED I was Jewish from the minister's daughter who lived across the street. At five, she was a year older than I was and had proved to be a reliable source in the past, teaching me both the F-word and its definition. I knew she was telling me the truth. I just didn't know what it meant. Because she said "You're a *Jewish*" in the same tone that she'd told me "You're a *fuck-you*" a week earlier, I gathered it was something vaguely bad, but that was all I had to go on.

As I had the previous week, I trotted home and repeated what I'd just heard to my mother. "I swear, I've just about had it with that girl," my mother sighed, jabbing a trowel into a bed of marigolds. "But yes. You're Jewish."

I waited for some elaboration.

"You want to know what that means? It means that you'll

never be good at sports and that you'll score pretty well on a test called the SAT. It means you'll always choose Tab over beer. It also means that we probably shouldn't be feeding you pork and teaching you Christmas carols, but what can you do?"

She tousled my hair and returned to her marigolds. "Don't look so worried. Nothing's going to change. Not until we have to start waxing that Eastern European mustache." She smiled optimistically. "Let's just hope you got my genes in that department."

My mother went on to explain that, in fact, the minister's daughter was only half right. I was half Jewish. Like the previous week's F-word discussion, this explanation began with a man and a woman falling in love and involved the awkward placement of body parts and other things that I wouldn't understand until I was much, much older. My Catholic RN mother and Jewish MD father had been working at San Francisco General Hospital. In between extracting baby-food jars and produce from the rectums of the sexual revolution's soldiers, they had managed to meet and eventually marry. It was a romantic beginning, and every time they hear a story about a foreign object lodged in someone's anus, I imagine they share a secret smile.

My parents have, in fact, been married three times, which is a lot for people who've never had their own TV series. The first ceremony was spare and secular, a formality, just the two of them and a judge. The second one, performed a week later, was trickier. At the time, my father was stationed overseas in the air force. It's difficult enough to find a priest and a rabbi willing to perform a joint interfaith ceremony in America; in Okinawa, in 1968, it was all but impossible. The priest dropped out when my father refused to sign a document promising any male offspring would be left uncircumcised. For my father, not only a Jew but a surgeon, this was unthinkable. Of course he would lop off the foreskin, and his future children would be lucky if he stopped there. He was always taking scalpels to us, removing moles and skin tags and infected toenails. This is how he showed us he loved us. "Just be happy he's not a gastroenterologist," my mother says darkly, arching her brows.

With the priest out of the picture, my parents turned their attentions to the rabbi. Initially he refused. My father doesn't remember what changed his mind; my mother insists it was her charm. Whatever it was, it worked. Thus, wedding number two. This time there were more people — twelve — and a fish platter. Following the ceremony, they sent out an announcement, a black-and-white photo of the two of them looking for all the world like a pair of lost Mod Squad members. There's my father in a three-piece suit, holding an umbrella over my mother, barefoot in a caftan and granny glasses. The caption deadpanned, "On August 30, 1968, Alain Traig and Judith Conroy were married. Wahoo."

Wahoo. And thus they settled into a comfortable life off-base in the bungalow they shared with a host of geckos and cockroaches. They spent their days treating GIs for the urogenital souvenirs they acquired on shore leave, their nights toasting their union over cocktails and Stan Getz. The evenings were balmy, and as the sun went down, the house filled with the scent of "night soil," an Okinawan phenomenon caused by the locals' habit of defecating in the fields.

If my parents had come from two different worlds, they were now in a third so different it made their own religious differences seem negligible. How to communicate with their lunatic Japanese gardener? Left to his own devices he urinated on the lawn and filled the flower bed with wilting stems cut from the neighbor's yard. The only English he knew was "Habu snake!" a phrase he hissed endlessly, jabbing two fingers in the air in a gesture meant to ward the creature off. It was a useful vocabulary but a very limited one, and my mother's pleas to stop watering the grass with his own hose went uncomprehended.

Still, their Okinawan neighbors tried to make them feel at home. Plenty of Americans had passed through before, and the locals had become quite familiar with American customs. On October 31 swarms of kids showed up to pound on the door. "American Halloween," they said. "You give us candy now." Because their previous American visitors had also taught them the adage "You all look alike," they kept this up for a couple hours, figuring my parents couldn't tell one group of twenty kids from the next. By the time my parents got wise my mother was scraping the last butterscotch from the bottom of her purse. My parents shut off the lights and spent the rest of the night hiding in the bedroom, their cigarette embers glowing orange as their ice cubes melted in the humid fall air.

It was a nice life, a tropical calm before the typhoon of family life. They joined the photography club. They shopped for cheap hi-fi equipment and the pirated records that would form the sound track of my childhood, the jacket covers with their mangled English leading me to believe, until I was ten, that the Breatles' greatest album was *Sergeant Peppep's Loney Heats Cub Banb*. On Saturday nights my father donned a ridiculous government-issue white tuxedo that made him look like Cesar Romero and squired my mother to cocktail parties on base. When his duty was up, he promptly threw the suit in the trash, and my parents' last view of Okinawa, as they drove to the airport, was of their garbageman in tie and tails.

The idyll was over. My parents had dodged disapproval and back talk by eloping, but after returning to the United States, they were fair game. They visited my father's family first. My grandmother was matter-of-fact and determined to make the best of it. She'd never gotten along with her mother-in-law, she told my mother, and had no intention of putting anyone through that hell herself. My grandfather said nothing at all. Though he eventually became very fond and protective of my mother, he would not address her directly for the first three years and reverted to Russian whenever she was around. "Tell Alain's lassie her scotch and soda is leaving rings on the coffee table," my mother imagined he was murmuring. "Tell our daughter-in-law her shoes keep scuffing the floor."

My mother's side of the family was a little easier. Oh, sure, there had been some concern when they found out my father wasn't Catholic. It's a favorite family story, in fact, and all these years later the punch line "She married a *what?*" never fails to get a laugh. But once my mother's relatives got used to the idea, they were fine with it. It could have been worse, they reasoned. He was Jewish, yes, but at least he wasn't a Yankees fan.

Now, a few years later, my mother and I were sitting in the marigold bed and she was trying to explain what this all meant. "Do you understand?"

Sort of. I was thinking of the song "Half-Breed," which was very popular at the time. It told the story of a young woman who was ostracized in spite of the fact that she'd gotten the best of two gene pools, the thick straight hair of her Cherokee mother and the fine-boned bearing of her European father. Against a thumping backbeat, she brayed her lament.

So I was a half-breed. "Do you understand, pussycat?" my mother repeated. I shrugged. At the moment all I was thinking was this: *I have something in common with Cher.*

I didn't understand what Jewish or Catholic meant, but Cher, I got. Her variety show was a particular favorite of mine. I'd seen her perform this very song and had been impressed by the feathered headdress and beaded cutaway outfit. She'd even had a horse. Did this mean I could expect a future of Bob Mackie gowns, Appaloosa rides, and turquoise jewelry?

"Do I get beads?" I asked.

"What?" my mother looked up. "You mean rosary beads? Oh, no. We're raising you Jewish."

So that's how it was going to be. I might be a half-breed, but there would be no half-creed. This was for the best. There are many things I fault my parents for — oh, how I wish they'd made me start a skin care regime when I was young enough for it to really make a difference — but for this, I am grateful. This they got right. It's the best solution to the interfaith dilemma: pick one religion and give the kids no say in the matter. Children cannot be trusted to dress or feed themselves; they certainly cannot be entrusted with dogma and doxologies. If I'd been allowed to make such a decision as a youngster we would have practiced a faith that required the liberal application of makeup and banned toothbrushing.

It was the right choice. I've often thought I was born into the wrong family — I cannot, for the life of me, understand how the rest of them live without cable or call waiting — but I've never felt anything but Jewish. That day when I was four, the minister's daughter only put a name to something I already knew I was. I knew I was different, knew the whole church/New Testament/communion thing wasn't for me. I was just too short and my hair was too curly.

"You're living in a dream world if you think you've never been baptized," my Catholic cousin Peter tells me. "You had too many babysitters and relatives worried about your immortal soul. Do you remember a visit to an indoor 'swimming pool' that had high ceilings, wooden benches, and colorful windows? Was the lifeguard a man in a white dress? Was he holding a smoking purse?"

I suppose it's possible. But if it happened, it didn't take. I have never felt any pull toward the Catholic Church, never felt stirred by saints or relics. I like those tacky garden statues, and *The Thorn Birds,* of course, but that's about it.

I knew I was Jewish even when I was put out by it. And at first, I was, as often as not. My introduction to Jewish practice came shortly after my tête-à-tête with the minister's daughter and it did not go smoothly. We had gone to San Francisco to visit my grandparents for the High Holidays, and my father had felt compelled to take me to synagogue. Perhaps my grandparents had heard too much Santa talk, or maybe my mother just wanted to get me out of the house for a couple hours. Whatever the reason, my father and I found ourselves in a stadium-sized temple where we had the special seats reserved for nonmembers who have neither tickets nor a twenty for the usher. From our folding chairs in the three-hundredth row, I could see the antlike figures dotting the stage below. The lush gilt splendor of the venue had led me to expect ballerinas or the Ice Capades. Instead, all the spotlights were on a cabal of wrinkled, bearded, chanting men. It was hot and dark and loud, and my red velvet dress was stiff and itchy. I glanced around for the snack bar, finding only a table of lukewarm herring. Clearly my father had confused his four-year-old daughter with someone else, someone like Henry Kissinger. This was just not my scene.

I fidgeted for fifteen minutes, then broke out into a full-blown howl. Half an hour later we were back at my grandparents' house, my father sporting bite marks and a fresh bruise on his jaw where my party shoe had nailed him as he carried me out. "Well, that went nicely," he announced. "I think organized religion can wait a few more years."

That was just as well. We lived in rural Northern California, where there was little organized Judaism to speak of. Even if the whole family had been Jewish, we would have had, as our farmer neighbors liked to say, a hard row to hoe. We were so isolated, ringed by backwoods racists whose hobbies included cooking batches of crystal meth and writing pamphlets denying the Holocaust. There were maybe six Jewish families in the whole town, most of them half-and-half like ours. Living next door to an Israeli family, we constituted the Jewish ghetto.

My father had always sworn that he would never live in a town that had more churches than bars. In our town they were in equal and plentiful supply, including several that blurred the line between the two. The church that interested me most met in a converted roller rink. I imagined the services were conducted under strobe lights, the pastor sermonizing over a disco beat: "Repent, you sinners, repent. Reverse skate!"

There were certainly more churches and bars than Jews, and there was no synagogue at all. There was, however, a Hebrew school at the Jewish Community Center one town over, and as soon as I turned six my parents signed me up. I did not particularly like it. The drive, over miles of bumpy country roads through hot, dry farmland, left me carsick, and the school's unappetizing snacks of stale raisins and off-brand Fig Newtons didn't help. There was a ditch next to the classrooms where the other kids in the car pool, all boys, could scoop up tadpoles and dead, leathery minnows to hold in their warm palms on the drive home. Week after week we sat plastered to the vinyl upholstery in sweaty shorts as the car slowly filled with the smell of decaying fish carcasses. My sister and I eventually built a game around these rides called Hot Nausea Car, a sort of bingo involving various emetics.

Still, I was drawn in. I felt sick and bored and put-upon, but I also knew I was exactly where I was supposed to be. I was a Jew, enduring Hebrew school like any other Jew. It felt right. It confirmed my faith in the same way that people who know they're gay remain gay even if their introduction to "the scene" is *The Birdcage*.

I would continue going to Hebrew school long after the rest of the car pool dropped out. When our religious instruction finally devolved into monthly potlucks at which we were encouraged to "rap" with other Jewish kids, my sister dropped out, too, but I kept showing up, tamale pie in hand.

It was all I had. Outside of Hebrew school our religious practice, in keeping with our half-and-half household, was half-assed. My scrupulosity hadn't come along to ruin the fun for everyone yet, and we still ate shrimp and bacon with abandon. On Friday nights, our only ritual was watching the entire ABC lineup. We observed the Jewish holidays halfheartedly, preferring the Christian ones, which tended to involve more candy and presents. Oh, we were careful to secularize them. There was never any Jesus talk, and the icing on the hot cross buns looked more like asterisks than crucifixes, generous frosting being more important to us than religious imagery — but they still weren't bagels.

Of course there was going to be crossover. Of course things were going to get messy. That's just how it works. In our house the commingling was compounded, because it was our Catholic mother who was in charge of our Jewish upbringing. My mother was the one who carted us off to Hebrew school and synagogue, who cooked seders and *sufganiyot*. Our Hebrew teachers knew we were half Jewish, but they assumed the Jewish side was the maternal one; our mother was the one who came to shul. Besides, she passed. She's got a Jewish first name and features. She is, in fact, the only person on either side of the family who's had work done on her nose. My father's Jewishness, on the other hand, was invisible, deeply felt but impossible to see. "I don't need to practice," he told us. "I've got it down already."

It was how he'd been raised, born to Russians who'd grown up in Manchuria, settled in France, then moved to China before ending up in San Francisco. Jewishness was their only constant. But it was a particular kind of Jewishness, a cultural one that relied less on strictures than sensibilities. It was fine to eat ham and to drive on Shabbat, but to put a bumper sticker on the car — that was unthinkable.

They weren't anti-Catholic but anti-catholic. Their aesthetics were particular but hard to parse out. It wasn't the Jewish American norm. They drank sugared sodas and dry wine, wore sunglasses but not sunscreen. Their Judaism meant shopping at Gump's but not Emporium, eating kasha but not kishke, reading Isaac Bashevis Singer but not Isaac Asimov. It meant doing things a certain way.

They had a large circle of friends whose tastes and background were nearly identical to theirs, eclectic as they were, but they didn't really fit into the larger Jewish community. Oh, they made a stab at it. They joined a synagogue shortly after coming to the United States. It was a showy Reform temple, unlike the Orthodox congregations of their youth, and they hadn't cared for the robed choir and English prayers. But it would do. They enrolled the kids in its Sunday school and made my father have a bar mitzvah. It was a glorious orgy of gifts, pens and watches and gadgets, most of them broken before the day was out because he disassembled them to see how they worked. His relationship with formal Jewish practice met a similar end. He learned the prayers and the principles, saw how it all went together, and put it aside. It was a nice thing to have around, but you didn't have to play with it every day.

Our mother, however, was used to great daily helpings of dogma and devotion. She had been raised attending parochial schools, going to church every week, decorating her bedroom with crepe paper altars to Mary. Her parents were devoutly religious and made the family say the rosary together after dinner well into the kids' teens. Every night they would kneel in a circle on the living room carpet, the girls' skirts fanning out like bluebells as they prayed with fervent devotion that none of their friends could see them through the open window.

Their friends wouldn't have cared. They were all Catholic, too. As for Jews, my mother, in childhood, had seen only three: two neighbors and a gentleman spotted at the market while on a trip to visit a cloistered cousin in upstate New York. "There's a Jew," her grandmother had remarked, nodding toward the young man examining the canned tomatoes. My mother was simultaneously horrified by her grandmother's prejudice and impressed by her perceptiveness. How did she know? Was there some secret Jewish signifier? My mother figured it was the horn-rimmed glasses, a belief only confirmed, many years later, by my father's possession of the same.

For the most part, my mother and her family enjoyed friendly relations with the few Jews in town, saving their true scorn for the Protestants. My mother's one-day courtship with a Jewish classmate passed unremarked, but her sister's Congregationalist boyfriend provoked an intervention. "If we don't stop this now they'll get married and have children — no, *child* —," my great-grandmother warned, "who will grow up thinking church consists of coffee and cake."

My mother's marriage meant no church at all. It had made her ineligible to receive communion, and she stopped going to church altogether. Having married outside her faith she wasn't in what canon law calls a "state of grace." Personally, I would have taken advantage of this condition to pursue some new hobbies, like gluttony or sloth. My mother filled her time with soap operas and latch-hooked wall hangings instead. She seemed reasonably happy, but one of her friends, worried about her immortal soul, began a campaign to get her back into the Church. It would be simple, she promised. She'd found a priest who was willing to "rectify" my parents' union — this was the official term for the procedure — and after that my mother would be eligible to receive the sacrament again. The only problem, she said, was that they had to hurry; the priest had been diagnosed with stomach cancer and she didn't think he had much time left. Were she and my father free on Wednesday?

They were. Hence, wedding number three. Twenty-five years later, both the priest and my parents' marriage are still standing; my parents' relationship, it seems, was the more chronic condition.

My father hadn't wanted to make a tsimmes of it, and arranged for the ceremony to take place while my sister and I were in school, not even telling us about it until it was done. This was a serious affront. I was seven at the time, and my parents knew my sole aspiration in life was to be a flower girl. I was annoyed that I'd been left out, and angry that my mother had forgone accessories. She'd worn a suit, a *suit*, to her previous two weddings and now she'd gone and wasted a third opportunity. I thought the occasion called for leg-o'-mutton sleeves, a tiara, a twenty-foot train. "What do you mean, you didn't wear a veil?" I demanded. "And where was your bouquet? Geez, what a crappy wedding." But there was cake and punch and a little dinner party, to mark my parents' third wedding and my mother's return to her faith.

When my mother started going to church, my sister and I did, too. This wasn't an attempt to convert us; she simply couldn't find a babysitter. She actively discouraged us from participating, growing alarmed when we picked up a hymnal. "Here," she said, fishing a horoscope guide out of her purse. "Read this instead." Still, it made my father uncomfortable, and he finally asked her to stop bringing us. He needn't have worried. The only aspect of church that piqued my interest was the kneeler, that ingenious red vinyl–padded shelf that flipped down from its nook, allowing you to genuflect in comfort. Man, was that great. I wanted one for home. It would be perfect for watching TV on the rug right up close, as I preferred, or for inspecting the welcome mat for dead bugs.

And it would have made a nice addition to our interfaith home, I thought, with its multi-denominational decor. On the refrigerator door there was a picture of Jesus made out of what appeared to be fruit leather, held up by a magnet from the Jewish Federation. On the mantel, a menorah next to a frond left over from last year's Palm Sunday. The front door sported a mezuzah and a Christmas wreath no one had bothered to take down yet. Oh, we tried to keep things separate and compartmentalized. My mothers' prayer cards and rosaries were tucked away here; my yarmulkes and prayer books stored safely away from the rest of it, there. But there was still so much cross-contamination. It was all a big jumble.

The anti-Semitic sixth-grade classmate who worried that my Jewishness was contagious was partly right, it turns out. We do rub off on one another. We absorb one another's credos, customs, cuss words. I'd say we bring out the best in one another, but it's more like we borrow the worst. My father swears like a true Catholic, invoking the names of all the saints and apostles, while my mother spits her epithets out in Yiddish.

I'm their child in every way. Though it's true that I've never felt anything but Jewish, I have plenty of habits that betray my half-breed origins. It's a fact that I drink Mountain Dew with breakfast. I watch Chris Farley movies. I can't stand lox or white-fish salad. I buy the wrong mustard and I smear mayonnaise on just about everything, even french fries. But I hasten to point out that this is a habit I picked up from my father, a man whose favorite snack is a mayonnaise sandwich. On *white* bread.

When I was thirteen I underwent a conversion to make my Jewishness official. But it didn't really convert anything, didn't erase my goyish affections or my gentile ties. It just made me a religious Jew who has a nun for a cousin and a Catholic lay lector for a mother.

We rub off on one another. No amount of washing would undo it, no amount of vacuuming would set things straight. Our home was a hodgepodge, a halfway house, and I sometimes felt I was being held there until I was socialized enough to assimilate in the real world. I thought I never would. That's normally the great fear with intermarriage — assimilation into the mainstream, loss of the outside culture — but as I grew older, crazier, and more religious, I felt as though I didn't blend in anywhere. I was just so weird. I didn't even fit in my own family.

This was largely my doing. If there was disharmony in our interfaith home, I'm the one who caused it. I was behind the

Easter Dinner Fiasco of 1982, the Passover Tableware Crisis of 1986, the Shabbat Refrigerator Light Bulb Feud of 1988. My parents had done everything right, ruling the house by dictatorship, a method that works so well for much of the Third World. It didn't work for me. Every day, I was stirring up insurgencies, issuing fatwas, declaring holy war on the whole damn family.

The problem, besides my raging mental illness, was that I felt cheated. As a child my favorite book was *All-of-a-Kind Family.* I loved those girls in their identical pinafores, helping their mother make honey cake and challah. It galled me that we were nothing like them. It was bad enough that our outfits didn't match. Having religions that didn't match was just too much. They were the all of a kind family; all we were was kind of a family. Sure, we shared genes, a last name, and substandard table manners, but other than that, what bound us together?

It's a strange thing, not sharing a faith with your mother, a person with whom you otherwise share so much. It made discipline difficult. What can your parents threaten you with if you don't share the same cosmology? After flirting with monsters and the bogeyman, my mother finally settled on Patty Hearst and the Symbionese Liberation Army. Until I was ten years old I was terrified that if I misbehaved, the SLA would swoop in and force me to accessorize with heavy artillery and olive drab, which did nothing for my complexion. On the other hand, at least the SLA family members all shared a common belief. At least they dressed alike.

But us, we were a mess, my father and sister and I subscribing to three different strains of Judaism and my mother subscribing to a different faith entirely. The best sport of any of us, she probably had it hardest of all. We supported her religious practice only when it involved tasty snacks for the rest of us.

It's hard. Tell it, Cher. We didn't move from town to town, and we didn't feel unwelcome, like we couldn't hang around. But boy, we had our moments. I made sure of that.

I imagine it's not always so difficult; my scrupulosity must have made a challenging situation completely intolerable. I know plenty of well-adjusted, happy people who are half-Jewish, just like me. Or not so like. For all we have in common, we have more that differs. That's the thing about these mergers. It's a strange math, the equation differing from family to family, from child to child, the outcome wildly dissimilar each time. Even in my own family, the sum varies, the parts adding up differently. I ended up an observant Jew, and my sister is a nonpracticing agnostic; my mother, devoutly Catholic; my father, baffled by all three of us.

Over the years we've figured a way to make things work. Mostly this involves keeping our mouths shut. We do not discuss our respective religions. Others are fair game, and we sure do enjoy a good Pentecostal joke. But Judaism and Catholicism are off-limits. We don't discuss the pope or abortion or the spread of ultra-Orthodoxy. Yeast infections are a perfectly acceptable topic for mealtime conversation at our house, but heaven help you if you bring up Saint Paul.

We all have our touchy subjects. Mine is my interfaith background. Though I'm unimpeachably Jewish now, there are still things I can't do, people I can't marry, royal titles I can't hold. The Hebrew term for someone like me is *ger*, meaning convert, or, literally, stranger. It's an unappealing word, a mongrel growl. Couldn't they have come up with a better term for us? Why not something cool and futuristic, like shapeshifter, or something glamorous, like Mrs. Eddie Fisher?

Maybe it doesn't matter anyway. As Cher sings, you can't run away from what you are. Over the years, I've stopped trying. I have come to accept the law and my lot. I don't really want to be king, and I don't want a different family, either. Sure, we don't share a faith, but we do share the things that really matter. We all enjoy pancakes, off-color jokes, and schadenfreude. When we get together, there's no fighting over what to watch: we all love *Cops*. And when the shirtless, inebriated perp wets himself, we share a smile and a knowing look that says yes, yes, deep down we're not so different.

Deep down, we're not. And if I could dicker with my birthright, I'd probably do something about my hair first. Oh, the hair. Geez, Cher. You don't know how good you have it.

PHOTO, SANTA'S LAP, 1974

The Good Book

M Y CHILDHOOD WAS reasonably happy, but it wasn't very exciting. Oh, sure, there was the religious mania, but on the whole that was pretty dull; I never managed to make any bushes burn or seas part. Like Bilaam's, my sister's ass could speak, but that was hardly a miracle. We had no signs and no wonders. But we could turn anything into whine. "This town sucks," I announced, surveying the lack of major retail outlets. "Our dumb pets don't know any tricks," my sister declared when they failed to amuse us. "There's nothing on TV," we moaned, "and we've never been so bored in our lives."

Vicky and I were completely incapable of entertaining ourselves, and our parents weren't much help. It's not that we didn't have ideas. We knew exactly what items would keep us happy and interested, but our parents rejected them all. A circus-trained primate, a backyard water slide, a child-sized Mercedes — the answer was always no. They refused to get cable even when I threatened to call Child Protective Services. "Nice try, pussycat, but subjecting you to UHF stations doesn't constitute child abuse," my mother said. "Now, if we were forcing you to watch PBS I'd say you had a point."

Ours was a hardscrabble youth of syndicated reruns and gardening shows, and my sister and I frequently endured long stretches of tooth-gnashing boredom. Sundays were the worst. In our house, Sunday was known as the Bored's Day. The rest of the week we could scrape together a few playmates or victims, but on Sunday there was nothing to do and no one to do it to. Every Sunday morning all our friends were carted away by the Bible Bus, a merrily painted wagonette that cruised the town snatching up children and hauling them off to church for a day of sing-alongs and Noah's Ark puppet shows. Hours later they would return, flush-faced and sky-high on doughnuts and punch. By then it would be too late to play, and they would stagger up to their front doors laughing at their churchy little inside jokes. What was so funny about Nimrod? Why did they crack up anytime someone said "Enos"? "It's a Sunday school thing," our friends said, wiping hysterical tears away. "You really had to be there."

Sundays were awful. The long day stretched out before us with nothing to watch but golf and Mexican variety shows, nothing to do but comb our parents' room for entertainment. One Sunday afternoon, after I'd mined their closets, carpets, and wastebins without turning up anything of interest, I turned to their bookshelf. Two volumes caught my eye: the Bible and *Haywire*, Brooke Hayward's account of her Hollywood family's descent into ruin. That neither one was appropriate reading matter for a nine-year-old didn't occur to me. Heaven and hell, I thought. This should be fun.

I spent the rest of the afternoon flipping between the two. Each book made a big impression, but unfortunately not a distinct one. Because I read them simultaneously, they remain inextricably linked for me and I tend to confuse the characters. Was King Saul the emotionally absent workaholic who left his family for Slim Hawks? Was Margaret Sullavan the young princess who found Moses in the rushes? I picture Noah and his family in designer bathing suits, hand in hand on a California beach, and I sometimes find myself wondering what chapter of Kings Peter Fonda appears in.

Well, both books make good reading, that's for sure. And on that first day I cracked their respective spines, I beheld all that was contained therein and lo, I judged it good. So *this* was what all the fuss was about. I read about Adam and Eve, and Leland and Pamela, and felt like I, too, had tasted the fruit of knowledge. Who knew it would be so juicy? Divorce, suicide, fratricide, nervous breakdowns, booze — this was spectacularly educational reading.

Several years later both books would prove instructive and useful, giving me an endless list of things to fear and obey. What if my parents got divorced? What if my mother grew jealous and popped pills when I started getting better roles than she? Was that spot on the wall a mark of the plague, and if it was, where could I find a high priest to exorcise the malignancy?

My parents should have hidden the Bible as soon as the scrupulosity surfaced. It was the only handbook to religious practice I had, and the idea that it might require context or interpretation was beyond me. I was completely irony- and allegory-proof. I read *Animal Farm* around the same time and found it to be a perfectly charming story about some naughty pets.

But the Bible, the Bible satisfied my every scrupulous pang. Sex, death, and impurity are the greatest hits on the OCD jukebox, and they are in heavy rotation in the Old Testament. Leviticus alone provides some amazing material. There's an entire chapter on *discharges*. Here it is, all laid out, everything thou hast been worrying over: swarming things and carcasses, leprosy and tetter, blood and sores and seed. Thou must not touch these things! The Bible says! And if thou dost, if thou accidentally dost, there are purification rituals that must be carried out with exacting care. It's all there, all laid out.

But it was so hard to follow. There were so many laws, and they were so weird. The sex laws alone. My high school was full of harlots. Would I be required to stone them? And what was I to do with this: "And whoever sits on anything on which he who has the discharge has sat shall wash his clothes, and bathe himself in water, and be unclean until the evening."

Suddenly I would have to determine who had sat at my desk before me, and whether or not he had had the discharge recently. Great. That was just what I wanted to spend my time thinking about. The Levitical regulations regarding bodily fluids are a rich vein indeed, and they troubled me greatly. Because I couldn't be sure what was issuing forth from people in the privacy of their pants, I regarded everyone past puberty as ritually impure. Everything they touched was tainted, and keeping track of it all was a full-time job. It was bad enough if they'd just touched something with their hands. But if they'd touched it with their backsides — if they'd sat on it — it was irretrievably fouled.

At school I only had so much control, but at home I could keep a mental inventory of all the chairs and cross them off as others sat on them. After a while I would sit only on the living room couch — reserved for company, it was the least-used piece of furniture in the house — and my special prayer chair, a torturously uncomfortable contraption of white wire grids that left a window-pane pattern on the backs of my thighs. From there I moved to the floor, which was fine until my parents got sick of tripping over me.

Later I would learn that few of these laws actually apply anymore; they mostly deal with ritual impurity that was an issue only in Temple times. But I didn't know that then. I took everything dangerously literally. My parents worried, with good reason, that I would try to make burnt offerings in the backyard. I *wished*. The Bible was written for a different time, one in which there were far better accessories. I just couldn't get my hands on the materials I needed. Sure, I could try to purify vessels in the Jacuzzi, but it just wasn't the same. I could try to expiate sin by painting the cat's forehead with ketchup, but what good would that do? I needed frankincense and handmaidens, shewbreads, goats, and first-born males.

But all that insanity was still a few years off that Sunday afternoon I first stumbled onto these highly educational texts. That day I was less taken by the signs and wonders than by the sex and weirdness. Like Eve, I was eager to share my newfound wisdom with a helpmeet.

"Listen to this," I said excitedly, holding up the books for my sister to see.

Vicky lay on our parents' bed, idly ripping the stitching out of the bedspread. She was staring glassy-eyed at *Fight Back! With David Horowitz*, the consumer justice show we watched when nothing else was on. "No way," she answered.

"Listen, it's interesting."

"No. You can read to me from that other book, if there's bad parts in it, but no Bible."

I shrugged and went back to my reading. We were completely different people, had nothing in common but a crush on Andy Gibb. It had always been that way. Only fourteen months apart, we are almost Irish twins, but we could not be less alike. I'm a dark-haired, pale-skinned Eastern European gnome, a short and fuzzy troll doll strangers sometimes rub for luck. My sister is a blond, a full head taller, with the capacity to tan. Except for bad manners and laziness, we don't have a single common feature. My hair is curly and my teeth, straight; my sister's, the opposite. Pore size, problem areas, general disposition — we share none of these. Vicky lets it all hang out. I tuck it in, straighten it, pin it back. I am anal-retentive; she is — "*not* anal-expulsive," she finishes. Anal-repulsive, maybe.

We don't look alike, don't even see alike. The first time we went to the ophthalmologist, he couldn't get over it. "Do these children have different fathers?" he inquired. Though I am nearsighted and Vicky, far-, neither one of us had any trouble making out the horrified and offended look on our mother's face.

By the time we were in school our differences had multiplied and magnified. I'd taken to school right away, had loved the stacks of fresh newsprint to scrawl on, the tiny cartons of room-temperature milk, the minions to boss around. Vicky's adjustment was rockier. It just wasn't what she expected. First of all, there was no TV. She had to wear underwear, pants, and shoes, and the dog couldn't come with her. Vicky had spent the previous four years of her life in her bathing suit, asking strangers if they had any gum and eating breath mints we found in the gutter. She wasn't prepared for this new world of rules and math, of cubbies and structured time.

She responded with nosebleeds. They came out of nowhere, these daily torrents of blood. "Have you been rooting around in there?" my mother demanded, inspecting Vicky's fingernails for evidence. But she hadn't. This was just a spontaneous bodily re- action to kindergarten. Some kids wet their pants; Vicky hemor- rhaged. It was disturbing, but it wasn't particularly dangerous, and after a while we got used to her coming home with blood spattered down her front and purple crust around her nostrils.

One morning she got a nosebleed that was worse than usual. I knew this because I could hear her calling for me through the par- tition that divided our classrooms. A few minutes later the teacher's aide carried her into my class, cradled in her arms like a three-foot-tall baby, feet dangling, head back with bloody tissues wadded to her nose, yellow hair spilling down. "She kept asking for you," the aide explained. "We didn't know what to do."

I didn't know, either. I was six. I couldn't fix this. And I was mortified. This was more embarrassing than the time my mother dropped a tray of cupcakes facedown in the parking lot and then picked out the gravel and served them to my classmates anyway. This was more embarrassing than the time the dog followed us to school, which hadn't actually been embarrassing at all, had actu- ally been kind of exciting and had afforded me a certain popularity for the rest of the day. "He just loves me *so much,*" I told my classmates when we spotted him through the classroom window, darting across the empty playground, a brown, panting blur. "He follows me everywhere. It's embarrassing, but what can you do?"

But a leaking sister, this was just bad. I ignored her for a full minute, hoping the aide would carry her back out before my classmates noticed what was going on. But she just stood there. Finally I went over and patted Vicky on the head. That seemed to satisfy all parties, and they left.

Shortly after that the nosebleeds stopped. Vicky adjusted, made lots of friends, got used to the whole routine, and did just fine for a couple years. Then she found herself in a class taught by a true moron. It's not unusual to see someone taking off her shoes to count to sixteen in an elementary school classroom, but when it's the teacher, there's cause for alarm. This woman's idea of social studies was to tell the kids about the previous night's date. For history, she recounted *Happy Days* plot lines. Art was pinto beans glued to a paper towel. She may have had a teaching credential, but she sure didn't have a lot of imagination.

When Vicky brought home a spelling test on which no word had more than two letters, and a couple had just one, my mother hit the roof. Vicky had spelled both *a* and *I* correctly, but my mother was still furious. "What's wrong with this woman?" she demanded. "The dog has tougher assignments in obedience school, and all he has to learn is to not mount his classmates. This is a giant leap backwards. If we let her stay in this class, in two weeks she'll forget how to speak and start making on the carpets."

A few days later Vicky was enrolled in a fundamentalist Baptist school. By this time my parents had made some odd choices, endorsing an all-salami diet for the cat and chandeliers for the bathrooms, but this was surely the strangest decision they ever made. Things were already complicated enough, what with the Catholicism and the Judaism. Handing Vicky over to the Baptists introduced a whole new level of crazy. The Catholics and the Jews have plenty of rules, but at least they both let you drink. Besides, it was unfair. Vicky wasn't the idiot; the teacher was. Send the teacher to Baptist school, to military school, to obedience school, but let Vicky stay put.

Well, it was done. And it wasn't like there were a lot of choices. Once my parents vetoed public school, it was either the Baptists, the Catholics, or the truly wacked-out Evangelicals. No matter what, Vicky was going to be wearing a plaid skirt and spending a lot of time in chapel. At least the Baptists were good for a rigorous education, and unlike most of the other schools in town, it would not include extracurricular tutorials in holding your smoke. And maybe the religious component wouldn't be that weird. Because our Israeli neighbors sent their kids there, there were actually more Jewish kids at the Baptist school than at mine. When Vicky left, I became the only one.

I was appalled by the whole thing, but Vicky herself didn't seem too distressed. Perhaps her month with the half-wit teacher had left her too inarticulate to protest or perhaps she didn't really care either way. It wasn't so bad; she had some neighbor friends at the school, and there was pizza on Fridays. There was also corporal punishment and a daily volley of brimstone, but you got used to that.

And so began the family's immersion in a whole new world. It was a world of needlepoint Bible cozies and prayer breakfasts, of gospel concerts and speaking in tongues. Our Judeo-Catholic background had left us entirely unprepared for it. Weeping statues and heavily fortified wine with lunch — these things were familiar to us; but not letting the kids trick-or-treat on Halloween — what was up with that?

Suddenly we were shopping for school supplies in stores with names like Psalmost Perfect and Kings 'n' Things. Suddenly my parents were attending PTA meetings that featured lectures on satanic cults and AC/DC albums played backward. My mother inevitably came home sighing and shaking her head. "What a load of crap," she would announce, throwing her purse down on the kitchen counter. "Don't get me wrong; I don't think that Acey Deucey business is music, but it's not devil worship, either. If you ask me, Neil Diamond is the one they should be worrying about. How else can you explain his tremendous success?"

They were strange, these other parents, and the children were uniformly weird, too. When Vicky started bringing her new classmates home we didn't know what to make of them. We'd never met kids like these. They were hippie Jesus freaks, born-again foster kids, scary backwoods children who spent their weekends burning tires and shooting rats. One girl's mother insisted the family's cats and chickens had mated. "The kitties got feathers," she swore. "It's the damnedest thing you ever seen."

Sometimes the children were cruel, and sometimes they were just lame. They were more or less like normal kids, I guess, but what made them so frightening was their conviction that Jesus was on their side. They weren't peeing on your bike because they were mean, but because Jesus told them to. They weren't eating their own snot because they were nuts, but because it made the devil cry. Oh, they were fun, all right. Instead of house or cops and robbers, these kids wanted to play Christians and Romans, apostles and proselytes. Even during normal play, Jesus would make strange, unexpected appearances, showing up, say, to battle Catwoman or to capture the flag.

They just had completely different references than we did. Their parents wouldn't let them watch movies or listen to the radio or read Judy Blume. Some of the girls weren't even allowed to cut their hair or wear pants. Many could, however, dress like hookers. We gaped in slack-jawed amazement at their tube tops, tight skirts, and spike heels. "Bible belt and shoes to match," my mother muttered. By fourth grade even my sister was tottering around in four-inch platform wedges and sheer blouses. Vicky wasn't permitted makeup, but her classmates, denied everything else, had full reign at the cosmetic counter. They came to class made up like baby prostitutes, the dainty crosses around their necks getting tangled in their heavily padded bras. Years later, after she was back in public school, Vicky would accompany her one remaining Baptist school friend to an out-of-town baptism that she likened to an evangelical wet T-shirt contest. "Why is Jesus only appearing to the stacked teenagers in white tank tops?" Vicky wanted to know, but there was no answer.

One afternoon a classmate of Vicky's rang the doorbell and politely asked if she could break our Parker Brothers Ouija board in half. Their teacher, she said, had told her to. Of course he had. It probably goes without saying that anyone who chooses to teach at a fundamentalist Christian school has a mission, or at the very least a bit of an agenda. My father would return from open house night rumpled and weary. "How'd it go?" my mother would ask.

"Well, it would have been nice if her teacher hadn't leveled *both* barrels of his evangelical fury at me," he would say with a sigh. "But it went fine."

Sure, most of Vicky's teachers were normal, and some were pleasant; there was one we liked so much she babysat when our parents went out of town. But others were *strict*. The school had a complex discipline system based on color-coded demerits handed out for various offenses; three demerits and you earned a paddling. It was kind of like skeeball, only instead of stuffed animals and ashtrays, you traded your tickets in for a really bad day.

The worst part was that demerits were given out for the strangest things, like for going to the bathroom. This made no sense to me at all. As long as you actually did it *in the bathroom* — an achievement my classmates did not always manage — there should be, I thought, no punishment. But Vicky's teachers disagreed. Perhaps the school's rule makers had confused eschatology and scatology. They certainly had some odd regulations on bathroom trips. One year Vicky had a particularly strict teacher who would not permit any bathroom visits during class at all. Most schools have rules governing bathroom use, but it's rare that they require frequent parent-teacher conferences to iron out. Kids began bringing in doctors' notes.

Vicky was not spared. She had never been bathroom shy, but the no-excuses policy just did her in. She started having panic attacks. She would try to get a day's worth of business done in the morning, making her late for school almost every day. The day after Taco Night, she would just have to stay home.

It wasn't a bad school. It was just bad for Vicky, a free-spirited girl from an already complicated religious background.

It was a lot to absorb. She pretended none of this bothered her, but clearly it was sinking in. Suddenly dinner was interrupted by announcements that we were all headed for the fiery underworld. "Three Jews and a Catholic," she muttered darkly, shaking her head as she looked around the table. "I wouldn't want to be sitting next to us when the Rapture comes." She began using phrases like "everlasting torment" and "lake of fire."

Vicky became convinced that that was exactly where she was headed. One afternoon she confessed her worries to her best friend. "I'm afraid I'm going to go to hell," she whispered. "You are," her friend whispered back. "If you want to be friends with me forever, even after we die, you have to accept Jesus as your personal savior." That was it. Vicky got down on her knees right there on the pink wall-to-wall, next to the canopy bed, and solemnly accepted Jesus. That Strawberry Shortcake and My Pretty Pony had served as the witnesses in no way undermined the seriousness of the occasion.

Vicky didn't mean it, didn't really believe it, and still thought of herself as Jewish, but she was scared and she figured it couldn't hurt. At some point she even tried to take it back, but it was too late. Baptist school had changed her. Vicky was becoming someone we didn't know. It wasn't that she was proselytizing; she didn't really buy into the Gospel, and even if she had, my father would have put a stop to that right quick. It was the fact that she went bat-shit crazy every afternoon. During the school day she had to hold everything in — well, literally, but emotionally, too. There could be no tantrums, no outbursts, no eye rolls or heavy sighs. Forced to find a way to sublimate frustration and anger, Vicky began clenching her butt as hard as she could. Once she clenched so forcefully that she flushed bright red; the teacher, convinced that Vicky had a fever, sent her home.

It was all she could do to hold it together every day until three o'clock. As soon as she got back to the house, Vicky became a flying monkey, charging from room to room, inhaling sugar, turning on all the radios, all the TVs, as if she were trying to flush out everything she'd absorbed at school. No, she didn't want me to read to her from the Bible, she'd had quite enough of that all day. She wanted Foreigner, Journey, *General Hospital*, Pop-Tarts. She needed these things. They were what made her different from her classmates, what made her normal. The rest of them weren't permitted junk food or television or pop music. Guns were fine, but Guns n' Roses was a problem.

When Vicky asked to listen to a Walkman during the school's mandatory fund-raising jogathon, she was subjected to a thorough interrogation. What, exactly, was on the tape? Vicky answered truthfully: "Come on, Eileen." Perhaps Vicky's delivery of the line didn't emphasize the comma. Concerned, the teacher asked her to recite the lyrics. Vicky obliged, and that was the end of that. There would be no coming on Eileen at the Baptist school jogathon, that was for sure.

Still, the school wasn't completely culturally deprived. They had their own songs, and though grating, they were awfully catchy. They were much more infectious than the religious songs we learned at Hebrew school. There are no pop hooks in tongue-tripping dirges like "Gesher Tzar M'od" and "Oseh Shalom." But "Jesus Loves Me," "Father Abraham," and "Arky Arky" — those just get your feet tapping.

There were songs, and on rainy days there were movies, too.

At my school, we saw Disney classics and cartoons, but Vicky's classmates got more esoteric features like *Years of the Beast* and *Kevin Can Wait.* Vicky's favorite was called *Super Christian.* It was about a guy who behaved like a jerk all week, only to transform himself into a perfect Christian every Sunday. The point, I suppose, was that one is supposed to behave in a Christian manner every day, but Vicky just liked seeing the guy be a jerk. "The light's not going to get any greener!" he screamed, getting impatient in traffic. This film was popular with all the students and eventually led to a sequel, *Super Christian II.* The franchise ended there, before the fundamentalist equivalent of Richard Pryor or Ewoks or Mr. T could come along and ruin it with *Super Christian III.*

Sometimes, however, the movies were gruesome morality plays that gave Vicky nightmares. The subject might be a cheerleader who thought it would be fun to try marijuana, or an honor student who became obsessed with Dungeons & Dragons. The protagonists varied, but their fate was always the same: they got into trouble, they didn't accept Jesus, and they suffered eternal damnation as a result. The worst of the lot was called *The Young Hunter.* It told the story of an ill-fated hunting trip taken by a born-again young man and his atheist father. The father refuses to accept Jesus, and you can just see the hunting accident coming a mile off. But in a terrible twist, it's his beloved dog that gets killed instead, and in the bloodiest way possible. The old man eventually gets saved and then he dies anyway.

It was a nice uplifting message and it stayed with you. Vicky could not get it out of her head, and that, I suppose, was the point. The Baptist school practiced an old-fashioned pedagogy that relied on indelible impressions and rote learning. Students were required to memorize more pages than a soap cast. Every night Vicky sweated over the Bible verses she would have to recite by heart the next day. Walking by her room you were assaulted by odd snatches and scriptural outbursts. "Did you just call me the Whore of Babylon?" my mother asked. "Did you instruct the dog to rise up and anoint himself?" my father wondered. "He's licking his balls, so you got your wish."

Over time it became clear that Vicky had talent. She could retain and deliver a line like "Strong meat belongeth to them that are of full age" (Hebrews 5:14) with moving emotional subtlety. Soon her teachers were tapping her to compete in Bible bees and bowls. Though reluctant at first, Vicky eventually agreed. It meant she got to miss school. It also meant she had to spend the day with the parochial school community's strangest of the strange. Picture the kids you see competing in the national spelling bee. Now picture them blazing with evangelical righteousness, dressed in ill-fitting polyester suits with crosses resting on their ties, in wrap dresses and suntan pantyhose and sandals. Add some foaming stage mothers winging overhead and you've just about got it.

Still, it meant she got to miss school. She was good, too. Vicky quickly advanced from local competitions to the statewides. My family marveled. We didn't know what to make of it. We never thought we'd have occasion to use the phrase "preachin' prodigy," and we certainly never thought we'd be using it to describe someone with whom we shared blood. Then Vicky was asked to represent the evolutionist side in a highly revisionist reenactment of the Scopes Monkey Trial, and that pretty much put an end to the whole thing.

The debate was doomed from the beginning. Vicky realized she was in trouble when she wasn't allowed to make her own points, even salient ones like "No duh." Instead she had to read from a scripted selection of feeble arguments. "You say you believe the world was created in seven days," Vicky read. "But you also believe that Jesus loves everyone. That can't possibly be true. How could Jesus love a nonbelieving sinner — like *me?*" Vicky could really sell a line, but these were beyond her. What was the point? The fix was in. Even if the creationist side had been represented by a monkey — a monkey with a vestigial tail and human grandchildren — it would have won handily. As the debate limped toward its lame conclusion, Vicky grew more and more apathetic. "We are told, 'And it was good,'" she said resignedly. "But is this world really good, filled as it is with nonbelieving sinners like *m* — Oh, forget it, you know what I mean."

Vicky was discouraged, and my father was furious. Shortly after that my parents pulled her out of the Baptist school. The evolution business was just the last straw in a pile that had been growing for years. My father had been ambivalent from the beginning. I understood how he felt. My mother was fine, and my blond sister passed, but no one has ever mistaken my father or me for an Anglican. Obviously Jewish, he and I always dreaded Vicky's school events, half-expecting someone to wrestle us to the ground and anoint us with baptismal water, or to corner us and try to tell us the Good News. As the extracurricular activities increased, he'd grown more and more uneasy. The odd Christmas pageant he could handle, but a Bible bowl was too much. It was as foreign to him as child beauty pageants and ice hockey. No member of our family had ever been involved in such a thing.

But curfew-breaking and sassy back talk — that was familiar territory. Vicky was launched back into public school just in time for adolescence, and in no time she'd transformed herself into a surly kohl-rimmed smart-ass who cut bullet holes in her Esprit sweatshirts and spattered her tightly pegged jeans with bleach. Where did she pick this stuff up? It's not as if we had MTV. Once again, she'd become someone we didn't know. Personally I wasn't so crazy about the new Vicky, and the feeling appeared to be mutual. For the next six years she would speak no more than fifty words a day to me, all of them prefaced by "Hey, dipshit."

It has always seemed strange to me that so few siblings in the Bible get along. The first death in the whole Bible is a fratricide. There's Cain and Abel, Isaac and Ishmael, Jacob and Esau, Rachel and Leah, Joseph and the other eleven, all of whom make the Haywards look spectacularly well-adjusted. They make the *Jacksons* look spectacularly well-adjusted. Biblical family reunions require flocks of she-goats and wrestling matches; they end in false accusations and hard truces made over fathers' graves. The best you can hope for is the family diplomacy employed by Abraham and Lot: you go right, and I'll go left.

During our respective Bible binges Vicky and I had proven ourselves fairly incapable of interpreting Scripture sensibly, but this lesson we understood. This lesson we could apply. I went right, and she went left. If we were pointing in different directions, we reasoned, we were less likely to step on each other's toes. Each fall, we claimed our separate activities. "You can have stupid nerdy Book Club and stupid nerdy Service Club and stupid nerdy Computer Club," Vicky conceded. "Art is mine. Not so much as a stick figure from you; it's mine. We can both have

French Club, but at French Club events, *tu ne me connais pas, tu comprends?"*

J'ai compris. I went *à droît,* she went *à gauche.* Sometimes we crossed paths. We'd be at the same dance, me primly manning the refreshment booth, and I'd look up to see her slow-dancing, sticking her tongue out at me over her date's shoulder. At rallies I'd see her across the gym, sitting with her friends, throwing things at the cheerleaders. After school, picking up litter with the Green Teens, I'd glimpse her zooming by in a friend's car, the stereo cranked so loud it rattled my teeth. There goes my wild sister, I would think, and then I'd go wash my hands fifty times and pray for her soul.

I figured she could use a good word, not really having a faith of her own. Because she was taller and blonder, people always assumed she was the Christian kid in our interfaith family, like our parents each got one to raise in their respective faith, like they each chose the one who most looked the part. "No," I would correct them. "She's a *heathen.* She doesn't practice any religion at all."

It's the pets who got raised in different faith. The dog got to be Jewish, because he always vomited pork. The cat was christened a Catholic when she refused to work on Sundays. They kept their distance from each other, but when it came right down to it, they got along fine.

MY SISTER'S ROOM IS THE GATEWAY TO DEATH:
A TWO-COLUMN PROOF

Given: Let A = Victoria Traig's room and B = the dark under-world

Prove: A is the gateway to B

Statements

S1. My sister is pork.

S2. Fig. A is contaminated with porkiness.

S3. If I enter Fig. A, I, too, will be contaminated by porkiness.

S4. If I enter Fig. A, I will be committing a sin.

S5. If I enter Fig. A, I will die (Fig B).

Reasons

R1. You are what you eat (common knowledge).

R2. A vessel absorbs the impurity of its contents (Talmud).

R3. An unclean room renders the occupant unclean (Leviticus).

R4. It is an abomination to touch swine (Leviticus).

R5. Sin begets death (Proverbs).

Q.E.D.

Forbidden Fruit

MY SISTER COULDN'T understand why I was screaming at her. Until I collapsed on the floor in histrionics, we'd been having a perfectly nice day. We had spent the morning working on our tans and the afternoon watching soap operas in the quiet air-conditioned house. And now I was rolling around on the yellow linoleum in my bathing suit, howling inconsolably.

"You just can't do that to a person," I wailed. "It's not right."

Vicky had instructed me to open my mouth and shut my eyes. I don't know why I'd complied. For my sister, the lines between food, not-food, and potential biohazard were hazy and blurred. What other people wouldn't handle without gloves and tongs, she would happily put in her mouth or yours. As a young child she'd been fond of found candy, thirdhand chewing gum, and commercial adhesives. I had seen her spit out well-chewed

bananas and then eat the masticated wad. On more than one occasion she'd dipped my toothbrush in the toilet and breaded it
with cat litter. Now she was older and much more decorous, but
when she got bored there was no telling. I knew better than to
trust her, but this time she had seemed earnest.

It was a frozen grape. Vicky had just figured out that if you
stuck grapes in the freezer, you ended up with tiny, green, grape-
flavored Popsicles. It was a treat, a surprise, just for me.

Here was the problem: the grape had four calories, and I
hadn't budgeted for that. I had, in fact, indulged in a stick of
sugar-free gum (three calories) because I thought I was going to
come in under my calorie quota for the day. So now I was screaming, and my sister was backing away and scowling, and my whole
life was ruined because now I was going to be fat.

Sure, I spit it out, but still. I'd probably absorbed some of the
calories.

"Jeez." Vicky rolled her eyes. "It's just a grape." She retrieved
it from the fluffy bramble of dust it had landed on and blew off
the lint and cat hair. Glaring, she popped it into her mouth and
stomped off to watch the rest of *General Hospital.* I continued
writhing on the floor until I'd calmed down enough to consult a
back issue of *Glamour* to see how many calories you could burn
by flailing.

"Ith delithuth," Vicky shouted from the living room. "You
don't know what you're mithing."

That's where she was wrong. I knew exactly what I was
mithing. That was the part I enjoyed. Missing things, doing without, documenting everything I did and didn't eat — these were
my new hobbies. This had started four months earlier, at the end

of sixth grade. I'd gone on a diet, and it had quickly mutated from healthy positive lifestyle change into crazy obsessive freak show.

At first it had seemed like a great idea. I certainly had weight to lose. I had always been a pudgy kid, allergic to physical exertion of any kind, drawn to eclectic foodstuffs like cake mix and brown sugar eaten straight from the box. I was not big on restraint. I had realized early on that I was the Rhoda, not the Mary. I was never going to be the belle of the ball, so I might as well dump the whole bowl of chips in my lap and have a nice snack.

Every once in a while I would catch a glimpse of myself and decide I had to do something. My class picture would show a plurality of chins, or my pants wouldn't button, and I would embark on a diet. These were always tremendously unsuccessful. What were you supposed to eat when you were on a diet? I didn't know. Health food, maybe? This was the '70s, and health food was big. Because saturated fats and tropical oils hadn't become bogeymen yet, it was still pretty tasty. Yogurt was still full-fat, granola still loaded with hydrogenated oils and corn syrup. I could do without all the carob and wheat germ, but the rest of it suited me just fine.

It did not, however, help me lose weight, but that was fine, too. Losing weight wasn't the point. I was really only dieting for the material. I loved discussing food and weight loss with my mother's friends. It gave me an opportunity to talk like Erma Bombeck, whom I very much admired. "Tell me about it." I nodded knowingly, age nine. "I even *look* at a Danish, I bloat up like Shelley Winters."

By the time I was eleven I was what department stores delicately term "Pretty Plus" and what my sister called "Fatty, fatty, two-by-four." She couldn't help herself. She tried out several nicknames before settling on Sister Infinity Fats. I don't know if this was an oblique reference to my burgeoning interest in religion or to my burgeoning obliques, but it stuck.

I didn't get it. It didn't even make sense. How was it funny? Even my parents thought it was hysterical. They told Vicky to lay off, but they were too amused to ban its use outright. I would occasionally catch them muttering the phrase under their breath and laughing. Sister Infinity Fats, hoo wee, that's rich.

In any case, it was true. I was chunky. I was wearing my hair long and straight at the time, and with my berets, I looked remarkably like Sam Kinison. Because I'd gotten too big for almost all my clothes, I was dressing like him, too. By sixth grade the only pants that fit were a pair of pleated gabardine slacks a teenage babysitter had handed down. I wore them every day, rolled up because I would not permit my mother to hem them, as I perceived this as some sort of defeat. Fat was one thing, but short and fat was too much.

After a few weeks of this my mother took me shopping for some Pretty Plus honest-to-goodness fat-girl clothes. That bothered me, of course, but not enough to give up my daily snack of butter.

Then, several months later, I started losing weight. It wasn't as if I planned it. I think I'd caught a late-spring flu. I hadn't been able to eat much for a few days, and when it was over, I was surprised to find that my pleated gabardine pants were looser. Huh. I'd lost a couple pounds. Goodness knows I'll never be able to get off to a start like this again, I thought; might as well keep going.

By the beginning of June it was an all-out diet. Summer vacation had begun, and I had lots of time to transform my little lark into a full-blown clinical disorder, a consuming obsession, ha ha. Soon my entire day revolved around eating. There was nothing but food, waiting for food, reading and writing and thinking about food. I spent hours planning my meals, leafing through magazines and calorie counters to come up with new dietetic treats. Why have toast (170 calories) when you could enjoy a toasted rice cake (40 calories)? Why drink a fattening milkshake (300 calories) when there was diet Dr Pepper, skim milk, and crushed ice (30 calories)? Why not subsist on raw zucchini sticks and mustard? Why not have gum for breakfast?

It was extraordinarily boring, this new hobby. I spent the better part of my day draped faceup over the Eames ottoman, counting the minutes until my next scheduled feeding, spinning in the hopes that nausea would make me less hungry. When mealtime finally arrived I stretched it out as long as possible, consuming my grapefruit and egg whites nibble by nibble, chewing each bite twenty times. Afterward I documented what I'd eaten, tabulating the damage with the aid of a calorie counter. Then it was time to start planning for the next meal, and the process began all over again. If I had any free time, I spent it reading cookbooks, drooling over the porny full-color photos of Lady Baltimore cakes and snickerdoodles.

Somehow I managed to squeeze an exercise regime into this jam-packed fun-filled schedule. Once or twice a day, I speed walked at a nearby park with my mother and her friends. Speed walking has never been a cool activity, but at the time it was entirely foreign. It was still an exhibition sport, and we were very much on exhibit. Cars slowed to stare at us as we whipped around the track, arms pumping, gluteals so rigid it looked as though we were using them to hold our house keys.

No one knew what to make of it, but everyone felt compelled to comment. "Hey," the neighborhood kids kept telling me. "Saw you, uh, *walking* in the park with your *mom*. Looking good there."

Yes. It was lame. Had I spent the summer eating my own psoriatic skin flakes, I wouldn't have been less cool. I didn't care. I liked spending time with my mother and her two walking partners, a perky nurse and a feisty German GI bride who gave great diet advice in a heavy accent. "You know vat you shoot make?" she confided. "De zoup vit de tomato juice und de cabbage. You veel loff it, I'm tellink you. Und it kips you regular. It fills you up, und den it blasts right out! You vill lose de veight like crazy. Just make sure you stay close to de potty, and don't vear vhite shorts."

And thus my twelfth summer ticked by, lap by lap, calorie by calorie, minute by minute. So this was adolescence. Judy Blume books had led me to expect a whirl of babysitting engagements and light petting with long-lashed boys, not calorie counting and constipation, but who cared. It worked. By the end of July I was thin. I was scrawny.

I didn't recognize myself. It was strange, the hollows and points that revealed themselves as the weight came off. I was fascinated by my hip bones, my clavicle, the knobs in my wrists and knees. Suddenly there were all these body parts I hadn't noticed before. It was exciting. I went to bed wondering what feature would surface next. Perhaps cheekbones or some useful new appendage, like a tiny third arm I could use as a coat hook.

Other changes were more troubling. I was disappointed to discover I had an itty-bitty head. My birthday picture that year shows me with my skin stretched tight across my face, my head no larger than the scoop of light ice cream (90 calories) on my fat-free angel food cake (100 calories).

Still, it was better than a fat ass. After all, I was about to start junior high, about to be dumped into a cruel and lawless society. Worse, the television was suddenly inundated with ads for a new diet center whose owner had a name remarkably similar to mine.

I have never been called anything but Jenny, and my life had been just great until 1982. Suddenly this near-namesake was everywhere, urging America to shed its excess flab. I could picture the next six years of my life, and they looked like this:

"Jenny Traig, you need to call Jenny *Craig*."

There was no way I'd survive. I was going to school with one girl named Christy Buttsick and another named Karen Vaginos, but I knew I'd have a harder time than either of them. My choices were to lose weight or to start studying for my GED.

So this sudden weight loss was a blessing. By the time Jenny Craig had saturated the junior high consciousness, I was already painfully thin. Classmates tried to make Jenny Craig jokes once or twice, but it didn't really work. I'd done away with the punch line. The gag would peter out: "Uhh . . . Jenny Craig . . . looks like you've already been there . . . uh, yeah." Besides, there were plenty of other things to tease me about. My tiny head, for one.

I'd been hoping for a swelled one. A few of my mother's friends had lost a lot of weight and afterward they'd beamed with pride. "I just feel fantastic," they said. "It's like I've stepped out of a cocoon. A cocoon of fat. Now I'm a beautiful butterfly. And I know I'll never be fat again, because nothing tastes as good as being thin feels."

I didn't think it felt so hot. It was frightening, being this small. Before, I'd been big enough to take on anyone. Now that I was going to school with hulking ninth-graders, with kids whose beards were so heavy they had to shave between classes, I was too small to protect myself.

I was also freezing. Without the extra layer of fat I was cold all the time. My parents kept the thermostat set to a balmy 60 degrees. Years later, when my parents dropped several sizes on a stint in Weight Watchers, they would issue a formal apology for keeping it so cold. "We had no idea," they swore. "It's a wonder you didn't use your bedroom furniture for kindling."

It was turning into a miserable year. I was cold and unhappy and obsessed with food. At this point I didn't particularly want to lose any more weight, but I couldn't stop. I had learned to take satisfaction in lack, in the spaces between my ribs, in the things I denied myself. Why would I stop? I was so good at it. We could have charged admission.

Or maybe we couldn't; everyone had seen this show before. I was the first anorexic in my grade, but the disease itself was nothing new. I knew eighth-graders who subsisted on celery and ice water, ninth-graders who exercised three hours a day. We read books about it, gave oral reports on it, saw after-school movies about it. I loved nothing more than made-for-TV dramas, but I was a little embarrassed to be starring in my own. It was all there, all the tired touchstones and topoi. Cue the scene of me examining my vertebrae in the mirror, of me crying at the dinner table, of my parents pleading with me to eat, of my sister tearfully apologizing for calling me fat, asking if this was all her fault.

Cue the anthropological analysis. I was trying to be perfect, like the girls in the magazines. I was ashamed of all I had and I felt too guilty to eat. I was trying to take up less space in the world. Or: I was trying to delay puberty, to make myself sexless, scared that if I opened my mouth for a grape, Mickey Rourke would follow with a shovel full of cherry pie filling. And if I wasn't scared of *9½ Weeks*, I was scared of nine months, for what was pregnancy except an exercise in getting appallingly fat? Or: I wasn't sick, society was. How ironic that my mother's family had come to America to escape famine. They didn't know that famine would become our national industry, that we would learn to market it, to repackage it, new and improved.

Oh, whatever. Eating disorders are unfortunate but inevitable, a rite of passage, expected among girls of a certain class. Of course I developed anorexia. Given my background, it would have been surprising only if I hadn't. There's a great tradition of the holy fasting girl, and an even greater tradition of the upper-middle-class overly self-conscious dieting girl. Anorexia is the suburban equivalent of getting jumped into a gang. It's like a bat mitzvah, only with fewer ice sculptures and more laxative abuse. It's a trope. It's a cliché.

Even at twelve, I knew this. It had already been done to death, and this bothered me. At least some of my previous compulsions had been inventive. But this, this. This was embarrassing. So it was a relief, sort of, when the disease mutated into something a little more interesting. By February I was starting to do things the girls in the after-school movies didn't. They didn't wash their celery three times in salt water, then carefully dry it on clean paper towels before deciding it wasn't clean enough to eat and throwing it out. They didn't hide Ziploc bags full of meatballs in their sweater drawer while they combed the Torah to see if it was okay to eat them. They didn't throw out blood oranges because they were convinced that they were, in fact, infused with blood.

I did. Something had changed. I was still obsessed with food, but suddenly dietetics weren't the concern. I had discovered kashrut, or rather, I had invented a new and super-sterile form. This was the master class, an advanced mathematics. Now I wasn't counting just calories, but things you couldn't see, atoms and associations and invisible demerits.

Now I was limiting my intake in an entirely different way. This was an extraordinary exercise in subterfuge, a tremendous feat of logic and dissection. Every meal was a puzzle to be pieced apart and rationalized. Behold, the dinner of meat loaf with tomato sauce, baked beans, and broccoli. This was my theater of war, with meat and dairy troops to divide and conquer, pork products to vanquish and defeat.

It was an excruciating and painstaking process. First, I would drink my milk just to get that out of the way. The broccoli was buttered, dairy, so that came next, but that was trickier. It had been buttered from the tub, which was just tainted beyond belief, loaded with not-kosher toast crumbs, contaminated by knives that had cut steak and then come back to reload the baked potato. There were probably whole discs of pepperoni floating in there too, but who could find them under the big chunks of shrimp?

It was a mess. I had to blot off all the butter, and once the broccoli was bare, I could eat only enough to evade detection, since it was so unkosher that I probably shouldn't be eating it in the first place. Then I would push food around my plate for twenty minutes or so, a pause between the meat and the milk.

"It's too hot," I explained, blowing on the lukewarm, congealing mass. "I'm just waiting for it to cool off."

Finally it was time for the meat loaf, trickiest of all, deadly but compulsory. It was crowned by a tomato sauce topping that my mother made, inexplicably, with a powdered dairy creamer, which had to be scraped off and moved aside. The fork was now irretrievably tainted, so I would have to drop it and go get a new one. The next problem was that the meat had been baked in a loaf pan that had been greased with generic-brand shortening, containing *lard*, actual *lard*. The entire perimeter was tainted. Only the center could be eaten, and of this, as little as possible, because it wasn't kosher beef to begin with. The beans were too porky to eat at all and had to be hidden under the meat loaf rinds.

"Very nice," my sister observed, clearing the table. "Once again Jenny has turned her dinner into a work of art." She cocked her head and peered at the meat loaf columns. "I shall title this one 'The Barfenon.'"

But as long as I ate at least something substantive, I got away with it. At this point I'd been so weird about food for so long that the new weirdness went largely unnoticed. And my parents had given up on table manners long ago. We came to dinner in our bathing suits, sat on our feet, chewed with our mouths open, and belched at will. Only once did they actually banish one of us from the table. My sister was five and newly enamored of a rather colorful phrase. She was sent to finish her dinner down the hall. "If you're going to use bathroom words at the dinner table, then you can eat your dinner in the bathroom," my mother shouted after her. For Vicky this wasn't a punishment but a novel pleasure. The neighbors happened to drop by in the middle of this and were baffled to find my sister sitting on the bath mat with her plate on the toilet seat, happily shoveling down her supper.

But some picking and stalling, that was fine. For months, my parents didn't ask and I didn't offer. To come right out and say it was unthinkable. Keeping kosher was so embarrassing and strange. My father had already put the kibosh on my earlier attempts to become a fruitarian, to go macrobiotic, to subsist on nothing but Alba shakes and fun-size candy bars. There was no way he was going to endorse kashrut.

Even if he had, even if we'd approached the whole process sanely, keeping kosher properly would have been impossible. In the early '80s, in rural California, there just wasn't much kosher food available. You could get pickles and raisins and little else. People hadn't gotten uptight about animal fats yet, and there was still lard and beef tallow in just about everything. In a civilized society you expect cereal and juice to be meat-free, but in 1983 that just wasn't the case. There was meat in ice cream and frosting, in potato chips and pancake mix. Oh, not a lot, sure, but it was the little amounts that bothered me.

Was it because I had shrunk? I had lost all this weight. I was moving in the wrong direction, getting smaller, and my focus had shrunk, too. Now I had eyes only for details, specks, fine print. I lost interest in paperbacks and began reading packaging instead, studying ingredient lists with myopic fascination.

Soon I was spending all my free time looking up food additives in the encyclopedia. Most teens liked *Tiger Beat*. I was more interested in propylene glycol, sodium stearoyl lactylate, carrageenan, and xanthan gum. The things that could be in your food! The carmine that colored fruit punch, it turned out, was derived from lice. There were calf enzymes in cheese, snouts and sawdust in luncheon meat. I began writing exposés for the school newspaper on subjects like "Jerky: What You Don't Know *Can* Hurt You" and "The Truth About Corn Dogs."

It was around this time that I took to calling restaurants. At home, I could see my mother preparing dishes so I knew exactly what had been contaminated by tallow or broth, what had been baked in the pan where we once found a dead spider and hence was inedible. But in a restaurant they could be basting the lettuce with clam juice for all I knew. It was possible. I'd heard stories. It was widely rumored that the disgruntled busboys at one local establishment peed in the minestrone.

What concerned me most, however, were not the bodily fluids that went into the food but the ones that went onto the pans. Were they greasing them, and if so, were they using a nice, hygienic, vegetable-based spray like Pam, or did they reach right for the treyf and hepatitis-contaminated suet? I was especially worried about pizza pans and began calling pizzerias to ask for details. The employee who answered had invariably just fielded ten prank calls asking how thick her crust was and had no patience left for me.

"You want to know what?"

"What you use to grease your pans."

"Oh, we use K-Y, just like Julia Child. When we run low on

that we borrow a little motor oil from the delivery van. Okay? And if you call here again, I'm phoning the cops."

The anorexia had been plenty annoying for everyone, but my new condition was even more irritating. I regretted that, but everything else about it captivated and absorbed me. Scrupulosity was anorexia amplified, anorexia applied to every area of life. Anorexics only worried about food. I worried about shampoo, shoe polish, water, air. Dust. What if some dust got in my mouth? Dust was composed of skin flakes, I knew, and human skin wasn't kosher. It probably didn't have any calories, sure, but what good is that when you're going to hell?

Anorexia and scrupulosity are, in fact, fairly closely related. They are both obsessive-compulsive spectrum disorders, treatable with the same medications, one an almost logical extension of the other. My severe bouts of scrupulosity were always immediately preceded by bouts of anorexia, and it's not at all uncommon to suffer from both at one time or another. Simone Weil did, and the combination proved fatal when she managed to die of starvation at thirty-four. Saint Veronica died of the same thing at the same age, despite the fact that she allowed herself to gorge on five orange seeds every Friday. Saint Catherine, also dually afflicted, preferred to snack on pus.

It's a strange thing, the eating habits of saints, told in tales that are not so much hagiography as gagiography. Oh, the stories: Saint Angela of Foligno liked to wash lepers and drink the runoff, growing ecstatic when the bathwater was chunky with scabs. Saint Marguerite-Marie Alacoque had similar tastes, relishing the phlegm and diarrhea of the infirm. At some point it seems it was fairly standard practice among the extremely devout to consume the bodily detritus of the lepers in their charge. This was especially common in Italy and France, which seems strange given the tastiness of the native cuisine. If an English nun chose, say, runny sore over spotted dick, no one could blame her.

But man. Pus. My eating habits were plenty weird, but the saints made me look healthy and normal. They made my *sister* look healthy and normal. But we had something in common, these saints and I, all of us weird in our own ways. I, Sister Infinity Fats, belonged to the same order. Instead of a habit, I had habits, but the principle was the same.

Scholars are careful to point out that the anorexia that plagued medieval saints was very different from the anorexia that plagues mall-going teens, and that's true, but they bear some similarities. What binds us are the fundamental links between faith, fasting, and food, the holy trinity of the female religious neurotic from Saint Catherine to Cherry Boone O'Neill. Who knows why these things hold such appeal? Perhaps it's because fasting humbles and purifies, or perhaps it's just because it fosters a cheap and easy high.

Or maybe it's just because, hell, we like getting our way. There is tremendous power in food refusal. Food, after all, is control. Anorexics are tiny, tanned Somali warlords, cutting off the supply of powdered milk and high-protein flour to the oppressed civilian fat cells. We are kitchen dictators, steadfast and zealous, righting everyone else's wrongs. It's a fantastic technique. We have nothing to do with our mouths but preach. Every time a girl refuses to eat, she one-ups Eve.

It may have been a brain-based organic condition that caused my weirdness with food, but it was the power dynamics that perpetuated it. What was the impetus to get better? For all the disadvantages — loose teeth, bad skin, downy fur — there were plenty of rewards. If you can keep the anorexia up long enough, you get *presents* for *eating*. Presents! And attention! My family revolved around me throughout my entire adolescence. My sister's occasional teen partying was no competition for my skeletal fire and brimstone. Valley of the Dolls can't trump Valley of the Dry Bones. I got all the attention. What was the reward for stopping? To get fat and be ignored, then go to hell when you die? No thanks.

My parents were tougher than most, always reluctant to indulge my craziness, but even they could only take so much, and I got my way as often as not. They caved. You want to subsist on breath mints today? Sure. Diet Coke popsicles for dinner? Okay, why not. And you need to spend half an hour inspecting the flatware? Fine. Sometimes it just wasn't worth the battle. It was never mentioned, but after my bat mitzvah pork quietly disappeared from the house. The transition was so serene and natural that it never occurred to me that this was for my benefit, and I was shocked the first weekend I came home from college when I opened the refrigerator and found an impenetrable wall of ham.

Without making a big deal of it, they accommodated me, riding out my flare-ups of anorexia and scrupulosity, accepting my grab bag of dietary idiosyncrasies. My mother quickly learned which margarines were parve, which brownie mixes were acceptable, which ingredients would make me fling myself down on the floor in a fit. When I became a vegetarian, she forged an acquaintance with tofu and seitan. And thus the dust would settle, for a time, until I relapsed and kicked it up the next time.

It was Atkins that put her over the edge. I still love my fad diets, and when the Atkins plan became popular a couple years ago I couldn't resist. A few weeks into it, I went home for the weekend with my Ziploc bags of sugar-free chocolate and nuts. I was fixing myself a snack of cream cheese with ranch dressing when my mother asked if I'd prefer tortellini or rotelle for dinner.

"Oh, neither," I answered casually. "I've gone low-carb."

My mother didn't say anything for a minute. I can't be sure what she was thinking, but her expression registered something akin to murderous disbelief. Had her thoughts been captioned, I imagine they would have read like this: "I survived your anorexia. I acquiesced when you decided to keep kosher. I accepted the vegetarianism. I supported you even when you would eat nothing but dried fruit and untoasted English muffins. But this is a bridge too far. Pasta is all I have left. You will eat it, and you will like it."

"Tortellini or rotelle?" she repeated, glaring hard.

"Tortellini," I recovered. "And I'll make the garlic bread."

It was a nice meal. The water glasses could have been a little cleaner, but we drank out of them anyway. No one got sick. No one got fat. No one got condemned to hell. For dessert, there was ice cream, and we all had a very nice time.

SKINNY TOMATO QUICHE FROM THE KOSHER GOURMET

This recipe is guaranteed to please even the pickiest eater. Glatt kosher and calorie-conscious, it suits any diet. It's a real palate-pleaser too. *B'tayavon!*

PREPARATION TIME: 6 hours
Serves: 4

You will need:

Paper towels (4 rolls)	*8 ounces grated cheese*
Store-bought frozen piecrust	*4 tomatoes*
4 dozen eggs	*1 teaspoon salt*
Plastic fork	*Aluminum foil*
¾ cup milk	*Paper napkins*
12 plastic cups	*Plastic knife*

1. Begin with a thorough hand-washing using plenty of hot water (see page 21 for technique). Once your hands are clean and dry, you'll prepare your work area. Lay down eight layers of paper towels. If possible, start with a brand-new roll (previously opened rolls may be contaminated). Be sure to discard the first few sheets, as the glue that seals the roll may contain unkosher ingredients. You will probably need to repeat the washing procedure after disposing of these first few sheets, as accidental contact with the glued parts may occur. It may take a few tries to get everything right. Take your time.

2. Remove store-bought piecrust from freezer. No problem here: it's certified kosher with a good hecksher and it's well-sealed. Oh. But it's been sitting next to an unkosher pot roast. It may have absorbed some juices. Better play it safe. Return piecrust to freezer, wash hands, then drive to the grocery store and buy a new one. On the way home, circle the same block five times to make sure you didn't hit a pedestrian. When you get home, rewash your hands and place new piecrust, still sealed, on a paper towel. While it thaws, proceed to Step 3.

3. Remove eggs, milk, and cheese from the refrigerator, being careful not to touch the door handle, as it is contaminated. Place items on paper towels. But wait. Maybe you accidentally touched the door handle without noticing. You don't remember touching it, but it's certainly possible. Better wash your hands again. Then break eggs one by one into the plastic cups and carefully inspect for blood spots before transferring to a new disposable mixing bowl. Don't hesitate to toss an egg if there's any speck of anything or if it just doesn't feel right. You only need three eggs. Surely with four dozen to sort through, you can find three good ones. Beat lightly with a disposable plastic fork.

4. Pour approximately ¾ cup milk into a plastic cup. Oh, look at that. The carton was sealed with glue. There's no way that glue is kosher, either. The milk is contaminated. Throw out the milk and the plastic cup and wash hands thoroughly. It's okay; you can substitute water instead. Measure out ¾ cup water into a new plastic cup, being sure not to let the cup touch the spigot, which is contaminated. This may take a few tries. Once you've got your water, add to beaten egg mixture.

5. Open package of grated cheese and carefully measure out 8 ounces using a plastic cup. Before you add to egg mixture, question the validity of the hecksher. Cheese is tricky, and maybe this brand is not as kosher as it says it is. It probably isn't. Skip the cheese. The quiche will be both more kosher and more dietetic without it. Carefully seal cheese and return to refrigerator, again being sure not to touch the door handle. Be careful not to place it on or near a meat item, or even near a dairy item, as the cheese is now a suspected meat/dairy hybrid. Wash hands thoroughly.

6. Carefully wash four tomatoes in cold water and dry on paper towels. Next, inspect but do not touch the tomatoes. Do they really seem properly clean? No. They just don't "feel" clean. Perhaps they've been coated in an unkosher wax. You'll need to wash them in hot water to melt it off. But wait. If you do that, the heat will render the entire tomato unkosher. Instead, rewash tomatoes in cold water and dry on new paper towels. Then carefully peel off tomato skin, washing knife between each cut. Be sure to use the grapefruit knife rather than the small paring knife, as it's the only one you know for sure doesn't get used on meat. Once tomatoes are peeled, wash knife again, and slice tomatoes into rounds. Add tomatoes to egg mixture. Stir in one teaspoon salt, if an unopened canister of salt is available. If not, skip altogether. Preheat oven to 350 degrees F.

7. Now you're ready to assemble your quiche. Carefully pour egg mixture into piecrust. Place the egg bowl in the sink to wash later, but wash your hands now. Then tear off several sheets of aluminum foil from a brand-new roll. Place quiche on the alu-

minum foil nest. Transport this whole unit to the oven. The top rack is preferable, as it rarely gets used and seems cleaner. When you open and close the oven, you'll want to use a paper towel on the handle, because it's contaminated. Bake for 45 minutes — just enough time to wash the bowl really thoroughly.

8. When quiche is golden brown, remove from oven, using a stack of napkins as an oven mitt. Place quiche on eight paper towels and allow to set for five minutes. Cut with a plastic knife and serve. Oh, look at them, making a mess out of all your hard work. Look at that. Look at that. Someone got quiche on the counter. You're going to be up cleaning that all night.

Today I Am a Manic

THERE ARE MANY things I like about Judaism. I like that it encourages napping and the liberal consumption of saturated fats, that it requires you to wear new clothes on some holidays and to eat cheesecake on others. But what I like best is that it endorses catered affairs for middle-schoolers. Judaism is normally a fairly sensible religion, but bar and bat mitzvahs are just lunacy. At thirteen everyone is at their worst, as unattractive and vulgar as they'll ever be. In a rational society, thirteen-year-olds would be sequestered until they were properly socialized and good-looking enough to circulate among the general public. But in Judaism, we declare you an adult, buy you a suit, then hire a photographer and a DJ to mark the occasion.

It's a recipe for disaster. Thirteen-year-olds pick themes like "Stacy's *Sex and the City* Soirée." It's institutionalized insanity, and everyone goes along with it. Give out souvenir sweatshirts embossed with the bat mitzvah girl's face? Sounds great! Put the pimply kid with the cracking voice and the uncontrollable erections on the podium? Yes, please! And why not record the whole thing for posterity? It'll be great!

It's a fabulous idea, the bat mitzvah. I knew by age eleven that I had to have one. I was motivated partly by a commitment to my faith and partly by a desire for formalwear. My Hebrew school friends had started having them, and it looked like a pretty good deal.

There is a two-year-long period in every Jewish preteen's life during which every Saturday morning is spent at a bar or bat mitzvah. It becomes a routine, giving the identical gift of a multifunction digital watch each time, evaluating the caterer's performance from one week to the next, debating the merits of Dan Dan the Party Man versus J. P. McGoodtimes. During the ceremony itself, when you got bored, you'd plan how to outdo them all with yours.

Because our Jewish community was so small, I had only a six-week bar mitzvathon, but it was enough to get me thinking. I'd also heard some stories. My cousins had recently gone to the bar mitzvah of one very rich and, apparently, racist young man who was carried into his reception in a paladin resting on the shoulders of four black men dressed as Nubian slaves. Another acquaintance had attended a bat mitzvah that featured a performance by actual Solid Gold Dancers and ice sculptures of the bat mitzvah girl in dance poses.

My mother warned me not to get ideas. I had ideas. Besides the bar mitzvahs, I'd been to a few big weddings, and they'd made an impression. So had several *quinceañeras,* the ceremony marking a girl's transition to womanhood, which were common among the fifteen-year-old Latinas in my hometown. *Quinceañeras* featured scores of attendants, with *damas* in hoop skirts and *chambelánes* in bolero jackets. We called them Mexican bat mitzvahs, but they were much more than that. They were like a religious ceremony, a beauty pageant, and a debutante ball rolled into one and held together by Aqua Net.

What I had in mind wasn't so fancy, really. It would be black tie *optional*. I wanted an hour of cocktails and passed hors d'oeuvres, followed by a sit-down lunch for three hundred. Naturally there would be a postprandial cheese course, and some sort of flaming dessert, if we could find a way to make it Shabbat-appropriate.

Nothing fancy. As for hair, I was thinking a three-tiered updo with French braids running up the sides. My dress would be easy. Any simple gown would do, as long as it had a four-foot train. I would also need a dozen attendants in periwinkle satin. I realized that this was not traditional, bridesmaids at bar or bat mitzvahs, but I thought it was a great idea and was sure to catch on. You could call them barmaids, or batgirls.

The next day we'd get a big write-up in the society pages. "Local Girl Becomes a Woman in Front of 300, Earns Jewelry," it would say.

Yes, it was going to be perfect. But it wasn't going to be easy. There were obstacles. There was the tiny matter of my father forbidding the whole thing. Bar mitzvahs were fine, but the bats rankled him. It wasn't really an antifeminist impulse. He simply thought bar mitzvahs were a gender-specific thing that proved unflattering on the other sex, like sandals on men.

My mother had been dreading the prospect of permitting me a platform and a budget, but this got her on my side, and after months of relentless badgering we wore my father down. I was going to have a bat mitzvah. Shortly after my twelfth birthday we made an appointment at our synagogue to get the ball rolling, just a formality, to arrange the date and the religious instruction.

The meeting didn't go as I'd imagined. I'd expected the rabbi would ask if I'd chosen a color scheme and a party theme and send me on my way. She stopped me before I could pull out my fabric swatches.

"We have a problem," she announced. "You're not Jewish."

Jewishness, it turned out, was passed down matrilineally. Since my mother wasn't Jewish, I wasn't either, despite my distinctly Semitic short-waistedness. Fortunately my religious status, unlike my proportions, was fixable. I would simply have to have a conversion, the rabbi explained. She went on to describe what this would entail — it turned out to be a fairly complicated procedure that would have to be coordinated through a more observant synagogue and that would, at some point, require nudity — but by then I'd tuned her out to concentrate on a daydream in which I accepted a standing ovation from my awestruck bat mitzvah guests.

"So are you up for it?" she asked.

Now the congregants were throwing roses. They were weeping, they were so moved. If it was going to take a conversion to get me to this moment, then so be it. I nodded. I was in.

My parents were less enthusiastic. My father was furious; my mother, hurt. It felt like an indictment of their interfaith union and, in fact, it was. But we'd already made a deposit for the caterer, so they acquiesced.

And so began my journey to Jewishness. My guide would be a kindly grandfather named Mr. Stein, who would serve as conversion coach and bat mitzvah tutor. I liked him right away. He had a very soothing presence, with his tidy gray goatee, crocheted yarmulke, and the enormous glasses that are standard issue for Jews over seventy. I was also very fond of his wife, a small, round, affectionate woman who was perpetually short of breath, with fluffy hair the color of circus peanuts. They were like Bubbe and Zayde, like fairy jewparents, sent to teach me how to live a proper Jewish life.

I took to it immediately. Mr. Stein presented a practical Judaism, not so much of ideas, but of actions. Not: here's what you should believe, but: here's what you should do. I found this tremendously appealing. This was exactly the kind of peer pressure I'd been looking for — come on, all the Yids are doing it.

It was just what I wanted. For some time now I'd been having these impulses to wash and check and eat funny, and now here was a channel, a vessel to give them shape. It gave me an identity. Now I wasn't just a weird kid; I was a religious fanatic. It could have been worse. If, say, an athletic coach had taken me under wing as Mr. Stein had, giving outlet to my determined impulses, I might have become a maniacally driven gymnast or ice skater instead. That would have been much worse. The hours were longer, and you had to wear leotards.

Instead of tights, I had Torah. Twice a week, I met with Mr. Stein, and he handed down new laws and lessons. We started with the basics of kashrut. Because food was a subject that interested us both, and because a little snack fit nicely into the lesson plan, we spent months on the topic. Just learning which animals were kosher and which ones weren't took weeks. In a less rural area we might have skipped or shortened the lesson, but living where we did, Mr. Stein knew it was likely I would encounter donkey meat and squirrel. These were out. Pigeon was fine, but not if you shot it yourself, as our neighbors often did.

Then there was the matter of separating milk and meat. This lesson, too, took weeks. There were so many substatutes and terms to learn. Mr. Stein brought in packages and taught me to read their codes, pointing out the *U*s and *K*s that indicated kashrut, the problematic ingredients that rendered innocent-looking products inedible. Both meat and milk had aliases, it turned out. Milk could hide as "casein," "sodium stearoyl lactylate," or "whey." Meat could be "mono- and diglycerides" or "natural flavors." You had to watch out.

By the time we moved on to bigger things like commandments, I was hooked. This stuff was *gold*. Twice a week wasn't enough. I began studying on my own, following a self-designed curriculum based mostly on the works of Herman Wouk and the encyclopedia entries on food additives. Mr. Stein and I hadn't gotten to prayer yet, but I couldn't wait, so I just started praying freestyle. Soon I was spending the bulk of my day in prayer. The rest of the time, I combed the pantry for new foods to stop eating.

Yes, I'd crossed a line. My parents blamed Mr. Stein. They'd liked him just fine until I started throwing out all their bacon. But now he was trouble. Now he was a bad influence. My parents didn't understand that it wasn't coming from him; it was coming from a dark, determined place inside me. They didn't understand that this was inevitable. I was obsessive-compulsive. I had spent the last decade tapping bookshelves and frantically rearranging my stuffed animals. This couldn't have come as a surprise.

It didn't particularly surprise me. I had known for a long time that I would become observant when I turned thirteen. Thirteen is the age at which you're expected to follow all the laws. Up until then, you're not responsible; you can mainline lobster bisque on Yom Kippur and it's technically permitted. I'm still not sure why I didn't take more advantage of this by cramming in all the pork I could that twelfth year. Maybe it's because I knew I would have to stop. I always knew I was going to become religious. I just didn't know I was going to become crazy, too.

Mr. Stein didn't know it, either, didn't know he was handing me grenades that would continue to go off all over our house for years to come. He did not know what I was doing with his lessons, how I magnified and misinterpreted them to my scrupulous ends.

He did not know, when he casually mentioned that you had to watch out with yogurt, because it sometimes contained unkosher gelatin, that I would go home and subject the contents of the refrigerator to a yogurt witch hunt, a dairy performance of *The Crucible* in which all the questionable cartons were accused and cast out. He did not know I would go on to conduct a cereal probe, a cracker tribunal, a canned-goods inquisition.

Mr. Stein did not know, when he taught me the prohibition against wearing a garment made of mingled linen and wool, that I would refuse to touch anyone wearing a different fiber than I. He did not know, when he taught me that milk and meat required separate dishes, that I would decide they required separate toilets as well. He did not know that my family was one mitzvah away from sending me to boarding school.

They'd had it. There was discussion of ending my lessons. But we were almost through, and besides, I'd started getting better. I just had. There was that business with the behavior modification contract, and then things improved. By the time Mr. Stein and I were concluding our course of study with a brief tutorial on gleaning statutes, I was close to sane. I was still a little funny, all right, but I could get through a meal without inspecting the flatware first. I could get through a full day of school. I was stable, more or less.

This was good, because the next step in the conversion process was the most unsettling. I would have to go to the mikvah, the ritual bath. I was not looking forward to it. Despite my washing compulsions, I didn't particularly enjoy bathing, and I certainly didn't relish the thought of doing it in front of an audience. A witness would have to be present to verify that I did it properly.

The awkwardness of the situation, I hoped, would be mitigated by the luxury of it. The nearest mikvah was in San Francisco, a big city, and this conjured images of glamour for me. I figured the mikvah would be like a spa treatment, only slightly more spiritual. I would have a wrap and a massage, and then, when the spirit moved me, I'd take a dip in my gold Gottex one-piece.

In reality it went more like this: there was a vigorous pre-immersion hosing-down followed by a naked inspection from the mikvah attendant that was so thorough it resembled a girl-on-girl reenactment of *Midnight Express*. Then, still naked, I flopped around in a lukewarm Jacuzzi in front of people politely averting their eyes.

It was a very complicated process. Nothing can come between the body and the mikvah water — not nail polish, lint, dirt, stray hairs, or dental plaque — and the mikvah attendant was there to ensure I was perfectly clean and bare. This was my own personal nightmare. The last thing a thirteen-year-old girl wants is to have her naked body examined by a matter-of-fact Russian babushka. It's just such an awkward time. I was so modest that I couldn't even try on belts in the Loehmann's shared dressing room. An inch-by-inch going-over was torture. It seemed to last forever. She investigated between my toes and under my nails, under my arms and in my navel. I had to lift up my hair and present my neck. I had to open my mouth and stick out my tongue. I was just about to bend over for the cavity search I figured was next when she pronounced me clean enough and pointed me toward the water.

Now all I had to do was immerse myself three times while a witness ensured that I did it properly. This was handled with as much discretion and sensitivity as possible, but still, no amount of discretion can undo the fact that you're being evaluated while bobbing around naked, like a clumsy Olympic synchronized swimmer who's lost both her suit and the rest of her team. I wanted to die.

Well, at least I wasn't a boy. The conversion for boys requires a scalpel. Even if you're already circumcised, you still have to whip it out in front of the rabbi for a ritual bloodletting. And you have to go through the mikvah ordeal, too.

So I got off relatively easy. And now it was almost done. I was almost Jewish. All that was left were a few formalities, like choosing a Jewish name. Though I'd spent the past year obsessing over the most minute details, I gave almost no thought to this one, opting for the name I'd randomly been assigned in Hebrew class six years earlier: Zeva. I liked it because it sounded exotic and chic and reminded me of Zena jeans, which were popular at the time. I later learned it was an unfortunate choice, the Israeli equivalent of Gertrude. It's also an exact homonym of the Hebrew term for genital discharge. An unfortunate choice.

Whatever. All I had to do now was appear before a *bet din*, a Jewish religious court, whose members would quiz me on my commitment to and knowledge of Judaism. They could ask me anything. I was prepared to answer questions about everything from the finer points of temple incense regulations to the minutiae of tithing, but I still worried about flunking. What if they asked about the sex laws? I thought that inappropriate study matter for a girl of my age and had neglected them almost entirely. Or what if they'd been talking to my parents? What if they went off-field and asked me how I could reconcile my behavior of late with the commandment to honor my mother and father?

In the end they asked me to name the matriarchs and sent me on my way. It had taken a year to become a Jew, and now, in three minutes, it was done.

It felt strangely anticlimactic, such a brief end to a long, tough year. It wasn't like getting a nose job or a tattoo. It didn't make me see myself differently. I'd always known I was Jewish. Now it was just official.

In any case, the real climax would be the bat mitzvah, now just a month away. Traditionally the bat mitzvah is held on the

Saturday closest to the thirteenth birthday, but my birthday was in July, which is just too hot for an outdoor catered affair. We pushed it to September, when the only open Saturday was the Shabbat of Sukkot.

This was good and bad. The upside was that there would be a sukkah in the synagogue backyard. I knew it would probably just be a lean-to decorated with overripe fruit and an entourage of insects, but my delusions of grandeur allowed me to imagine it as a charming hut in which I might play milkmaid, like Marie Antoinette in her Petit Trianon.

The downside was that in choosing this Shabbat I had earned myself a real challenge of a haftorah, the portion of the Prophets traditionally read by the bar or bat mitzvah child. One of the longest and darkest portions, about the apocalyptic war between the mysterious Gog and Magog, it is baffling and opaque. The only thing that comes through clearly is a doomsday sentiment. It features waste places and pestilence, creeping things and earthquakes, fire and brimstone. It's the liturgical equivalent of *I Spit on Your Grave*. The melody is just as difficult as the content, marked by the rarest and most challenging of tropes. Besides having to repeat the tongue twister "Gog and Magog" over and over, I would be required to perform vocal gymnastics that are normally the province of castrati.

Well, at least I didn't have to worry about my voice cracking; at least I wasn't a boy. Still, I wasn't the man for the job. I cannot sing at all. My voice comes from my mother's side, a long line of tin-eared tone-deaf caterwaulers. A few years ago, at my cousin's wedding reception, my kin decided to see whose voice was the worst of all. The ensuing karaoke competition proved so excruciating that four squad cars were dispatched to shut it down. *Four.* With sirens.

I had reason to worry, but I hoped the backup singers might make up for my musical shortcomings. If not, surely the sound technicians could smooth out my rough edges. My mother snorted when I asked where the madrigal chorus would sit.

"Ha," she said. "If you want I'll hand out kazoos, but that's all the musical accompaniment you're going to get. Well, unless we have beans for breakfast."

All that work becoming a Jew, only to be rewarded with so little fanfare. Over the next few weeks my parents dashed hope after hope. The omelet station was out. There would be no Tiffany mezuzahs as favors for the guests. I could forget about the *amuse-bouches.* "This is going to be a *country* bat mitzvah," my mother warned me, "and if you push me I guarantee I'll back a pig on a spit right up to the synagogue. So be happy with what you get."

What I would get was a hot and cold buffet, an oversized challah, and mini bagels. There would be no champagne fountain, no sorbet course, and I would have to make the desserts myself. Instead of tails, the servers would be wearing clever T-shirts that made it look as though they were wearing tuxedos. Well, that was kind of cool. I could be happy with that.

The only thing left to do was write my speech. This was the part I'd been dreading and the part everyone else was looking forward to, for its potential comic value. Laugh with me or laugh at me — it was sure to be good. My parents wanted me to deliver twenty minutes of stand-up. "You can do it in a televangelist voice. You can punctuate everything with 'A-yesss!' and 'Can I get a witness?' It'll be a riot." My parents are lovely people but they had no idea what would cause a middle-schooler a lifetime of ostracization. They had also tried to get me to do this when I'd run for student council.

I wanted to skip the speech entirely. Although I enjoyed pontificating, I preferred small crowds. Public speaking had never been my strong suit, and for the talent portion of my parochial pageant, I wanted to do something else. Couldn't I do a little dance number instead? Couldn't I just twirl a baton?

I put off writing the speech until the last possible moment. At the rehearsal, four days before the ceremony, I still hadn't written a word. A synagogue member took pity on me and dictated a speech on the spot. I wrote it down, giving little thought to what it actually meant. It was five minutes long, and it mentioned Torah several times. It also struck me as perhaps a little political, but I didn't really understand it, and in any case I thought it would make me sound smart. It would do.

The night before the ceremony my father had the foresight to ask to see my speech. That no one had worried about this before was a gross oversight. I'd spent the better part of the last year obsessed with ritual purity and burnt offerings. Giving me a podium was a terrible idea. I could have incited the crowd to stone the caterer.

The speech was short, about three paragraphs. My father read it in a minute and a half. "Bring me a pen," he commanded when he had finished, his teeth gritted, his forehead a dark knot.

Ten minutes later he'd calmed down enough to discuss the issue. "'Kill all the infidels' is not an appropriate topic for a bat mitzvah speech," he said calmly. "The idea here is to thank your family and teachers, to tell everyone what you've learned, and to butter up the guests in anticipation of large savings bonds. Issuing a fatwa will not accomplish these ends. Now, I'm going to write you another speech, and you are going to read it, and if it goes over especially well we can split the take."

The next morning there were two more fights. Because it was Shabbat, I couldn't shower. Because the previous two days had been the first two days of Sukkot, I now hadn't showered for three. My mother was beside herself. "Your relatives didn't fly all the way across the country to see you with your hair looking like that," she insisted. "Well, I didn't spend a whole year learning Torah to violate it today," I returned. "Besides, the yarmulke will cover the really matted spot." In the end we agreed to a wet combing and a "French shower," a liberal dousing in cologne.

Next was a skirmish over the pictures. I didn't want to have my picture taken on Shabbat. But my parents' argument that it wasn't too late to call the whole thing off so I could spend the day thinking about how ungrateful I'd been was a convincing one. I agreed to pose for five quick pictures, looking aside in all of them while I mentally chanted, "I'm not here, I'm not here, I'm not here."

The rest of the day was a blur. I was too busy and excited to notice that instead of the linen-draped bamboo seats I had requested there were metal folding chairs; instead of rare orchids, carnations. What did that matter when there were so many people bearing presents? It was a fine day. My friends were all there, trussed into dresses and tights. Over lunch they performed a guttural and somewhat unflattering replay of my haftorah, kugel flying out of their mouths with each *"chhhhh,"* but I knew they were impressed.

Afterward, they came to my house to work on the leftover lemon bars and brownies. Apparently the euphoria of the day got to me, and by late afternoon, when a friend produced her camera and asked me to pose, I was loose enough to submit to the photo session that I had stridently objected to that morning. I hadn't remembered this at all until I came across the photos recently, but there's me in a polo dress, a giant Star of David around my neck, pirouetting in the backyard, hugging trees, lying on the lawn with my chin propped against my hands as I looked dreamily off into the distance on My Special Day.

I had decided to forgo the traditional Saturday-night bat mitzvah dance when my parents informed me they would fly in neither Jean-Pierre Rampal nor the brilliant studio musicians responsible for *Hooked on the Classics*. Instead, the evening's festivities consisted of sitting around the living room opening presents while my friends watched. Because none of them were Jewish, they constituted an extremely appreciative audience. I basked in their envy. They would have to get married or pregnant to get presents like these.

It was a respectable haul. I got some pens, of course, gift certificates and jewelry boxes, and coffee table books on subjects like the Library of Congress and the Dead Sea Scrolls. Because the '70s had just ended, I also got several copies of *Jonathan Livingston Seagull* and several more of its sequel. I can't imagine why so many people thought it was a good idea to give a recovering religious fanatic a book subtitled "The Adventures of a Reluctant Messiah." What were they thinking? Inside one copy, a friend of my parents had even scrawled, "I hope this changes your life like it changed mine."

I hoped it wouldn't. By this point I'd had enough change, enough conversions and transformations. In the past year I'd gone from ostensibly gentile to unimpeachably Jewish, from child to teen, from sane to crazy and back again. The mutations had all been so public, too, all requiring witnesses, an audience, an intervention. Today was just the last in what had already been a yearlong festival of very public transitions. Can I get a witness, indeed. I'd had plenty.

This, I suppose, is what puberty is. What was happening to me was just an exaggerated version of what happens to every kid: look, she got her boobies. Every society does this, marching you out right at the moment you want to hide in a dark closet and molt. I would say it doesn't make any sense, but in fact it's inspired — it inculcates a sense of shame that will keep you in line for years to come. And making sure these events occur publicly, in front of witnesses, is a good way to ensure you won't turn and start hitting anyone.

Including gifts is a good idea, too. Yes, there had been a lot of change, and on Monday there would be even more. Half of this crap had to go back. Who would buy a thirteen-year-old a travel iron?

But it had been a good day. By ten o'clock that night we were wiped out. We waved goodbye to our guests and stumbled to our beds, leaving the piles of torn gift wrap on the floor, the dirty cups and crumpled napkins on the counter. The dishes and thank-you notes could wait. It had been a very full day, a very good one.

As I drifted off to sleep I replayed all the high points. It really had been quite lovely. It had been great. But man, if we just could have had a cheese course — it would have been *perfect*.

GLOBAL EVENTS FOR WHICH I CONSIDERED MYSELF RESPONSIBLE *(A PARTIAL LISTING)*

1. The Soviet invasion of Afghanistan
2. The Soviet boycott of the 1984 Olympics
3. The Falklands War
4. The crash of the space shuttle *Challenger*
5. Ethiopian famine
6. Bhopal
7. Chernobyl
8. Three Mile Island
9. Mount Saint Helens
10. New Coke
11. The assassination of Anwar Sadat
12. The assassination of Swedish premier Olaf Palme
13. The assassination of all three Gandhis
14. The Iran hostage crisis
15. All North American kidnappings, 1982–87
16. The hole in the ozone layer
17. The arrest and conviction of Jonathan Pollard
18. The cancellation of *The Merv Griffin show*
19. Apartheid
20. Red Sox loss of the World Series, 1986

Idle Hands

THE SUMMER I turned twelve the country was seized by *E.T.* mania. Everywhere you looked, there was that lovable alien, on soda cans, on tote bags, on T-shirts urging you to phone home. I saw the movie once and liked it fine, but for me the summer was defined by another blockbuster altogether. It was a rumination, a mental image that ran over and over in my head. This happened every summer. I just get antsy when I have too much free time. Come June, images would start looping endlessly in my brain, an unspooling reel of torturous what-ifs. In 1982, while the rest of the country was watching *E.T.*, I was watching myself stab my mother.

I didn't want to. I enjoyed my mother's company and spent most of my day following her around the house. But the image wouldn't go away. A local kid had recently done that very thing, and that made it a million times worse. That he'd actually gone and done it — stabbed his own mother! — sent me right to the edge. Now we knew it was possible, and if it was possible, what would stop me?

I couldn't tell anyone about this. It was just too awful. My previous summer ruminations had been bad — I'd worried about becoming addicted to Carmex, about being abducted by bank-robbing guerrillas who would force me to get a traumatic yet flattering haircut — but they had never been about hurting someone else. This was so much worse. It was going to be a long summer, I could tell already. I'd embarked on a new eating disorder, but it wasn't enough to distract me from thoughts of violence, and every time my mother asked me to chop the salad vegetables I nearly burst into tears.

Finally, after noticing me looking at her funny for a few days, my mother announced it was time I learned to knit. I was delighted. This was a fantastic idea. Knitting would give my hands something to do besides knife family members. Of course, it would provide me with another, pointier weapon, but we didn't worry too much about that.

And we didn't have to. As soon as I picked up the needles and yarn, I felt peaceful and calm. It was such a relief, the needles clicking a soothing tattoo, the skeins unwinding like woolly Valium. Knitting instantly provided the same sense of serenity I could otherwise achieve only by pulling out clumps of hair. The two activities are so closely linked for me that I can't believe they're not etymologically related, the Latin *trichos*, hair, a near homonym of the French *tricot*, knit. As long as I was yanking on some fibers, be they worsted-weight wool or my own arm hair, I felt placid and safe.

This, too, happened every summer. There was an agonizing week of ruminating, an intervention by my mother, and then three months of crafting. This year it was knitting, last year cross-stitch, and patchwork the year before that. Weaving, batiking, silk-screening, smocking: I learned to do it all. By the time I left for college I was quite sure that if I ever got stranded on a desert island, within six months I would not only be alive, I would have launched my own line of handcrafted garments fashioned from the island's meager resources.

I am in most areas a completely incompetent person, but in this one department I know what I'm doing. I can craft anything. My friends marvel at my savant-like expertise. They have come to believe, because I have lied to them, that my mother raised me as a seamstress apprentice, forcing me to work in exchange for my keep and tutelage. My training, I tell them, was as rigorous as that of a young Jedi knight or, more accurately, a Karafte Kid. The first few years were spent doing exercises that seemed to benefit my mother more than me: organizing her thread spools, balancing her checkbook, washing her car, and the like. When I complained, she answered in cryptic Pat Morita fashion: "Cleaning out garage might teach student to shut mouth." Finally she deemed me ready for actual craft work and let me crochet her dishrags.

This isn't quite true, but then again, it's not all that far off. Ever since I could remember, my sister and I understood that the hot months would be spent in our mother's version of summer school. From June to September we would be inculcated with her passion for all things crafty. We might not share her religion, but we would worship her false deities.

While our friends took dance lessons and karate, my sister and I were shuttled to embroidery classes and quilt conventions. These were supplemented with plenty of at-home tutorials. In our free time we memorized patchwork patterns and knitting stitches. "Quick! Name it!" our mother would quiz us, pointing to quilt blocks with their names like yoga poses: flying geese, bear's claw, Jacob's ladder, drunkard's path. "What's the difference between a rice stitch and a moss stitch?" she demanded. "How do you make a braided cable?" She taught us to read color wheels, and in the morning she would shake us awake with swatches in hand. "Quick! Which is the blue-based red and which is the yellow-based? Think! *Think!*"

She was very serious about form and technique. Oh, sometimes we used kits, and sometimes we did lazy amateur crafts, making Shrinky Dinks and oven-baked stained glass panels, but mostly we learned to make things from scratch. "Machine-quilted," she would sniff, examining pieces that failed to pass her muster at quilt shows. We learned to look down our noses at unlined home tailoring and acrylic blends. In all other areas she believed in taking the easy route, but she insisted that craft work and pudding-making be done the hard way. No shortcuts. Except for the soap operas and swearing, we might as well have been Amish. We spent our days working on swatches and samplers, practicing needlework's most archaic forms. Cross-stitch was just an entrée. We learned bargello and candlewicking, crewel and tatting. Had we also been given pianoforte lessons, and been born about two hundred years earlier, we would have been quite the marriageable young ladies.

As it was we were kind of dorks, but that suited me fine. I was just relieved we weren't being forced to play outside. I knew kids whose mothers locked them out of the house on the grounds that fresh air was good for you. Surely these mothers hadn't gotten a lungful of the pesticide-rich oven-hot ether that hung over our California farm town. In summer, the temperature normally hovered around 110, and the air was as fresh and healthy as that at a Soviet smog inspection station.

But inside it was cool and pleasant, and the worst thing our mother subjected us to was macramé. Seventies crafting was fairly dismal, it's true. We latch-hooked wall hangings in yellows and browns using kits depicting the popular figures of the day — the Bionic Man, the Fonz, the Waltons. We fashioned clunky pottery whose leaded glazes gave us headaches. In the kitchen, we crafted our own granola bars and yogurt. What child wants to play with yogurt?

On the other hand, the regulations regarding toxic materials were much more lax in the '70s, and we got to work with substances whose fumes left us pleasantly high. Our favorite was a strange and fairly pointless bubble-making kit you could find in the children's section of any craft store. You squeezed a blob of malleable plastic from a tube and placed it at the end of a straw, which you blew through, transforming the blob into a bubble colored like a gasoline rainbow. This, in fact, is exactly what it smelled like. It was completely absorbing, between the fumes and the paraphernalia, and became very popular among the children of the '70s, preparing some of us for future careers as crackheads.

The brain damage sustained from using these materials may explain the crafty atrocities my sister and I created in the '80s. We put our background in classical needlework to good use Beadazzling our acid-washed jean jackets. We beaded armloads of Madonna wanna-be bracelets and spattered our clothes with Jackson Pollack–style squiggles in neon fabric paint. We stenciled carefully cut-up sweatshirts with new-wave slogans that urged passersby to "Chill Out!" or warned them we were "Bitchen and Bewitchen."

The crafts at Hebrew school just couldn't compete. There, our craft supplies were limited to burlap and glue. These two materials were the sole components of almost everything we made, from scratchy pageant costumes to charmless rustic wall hangings. On a good day, we might make clumsy havdalah candles or faded sukkah garlands, but these never managed to sustain my interest. They were dusty and colorless, lacking the spangly appeal of the things I made at home. I was, however, quite taken with the sixth-grade sugar cube Masada. I'm not sure whose idea it was to teach us this important history lesson by having us fashion the mountaintop bulwark out of coffee accompaniments, but the upshot was that we ended up snacking on the Jewish people's most tragic martyr site. That the cubes were coated in white glue deterred us not one bit. "It just makes it easier to eat two or three at a time," we enthused.

But if there was supposed to be some sort of lesson, it didn't stick. I never learned to associate craft with creed, mosaic with Mosaic. I just wasn't interested in crocheting prayer book cozies or tallis bags. I'm not sure why. The only working artist I knew, my cousin, made religious art. She was Isaac Bashevis Singer's illustrator and she painted lots of shtetl scenes, portraits of women lighting Shabbat candles and men donning tefillin. I was suitably impressed but felt no need to create ritual art of my own. In part, I was afraid I would do it wrong, breaking some unknown law by gluing pom-pom trim on a challah cover. But mostly I just wasn't all that compelled. I liked making things I could wear. If there were some religious paraphernalia that would go well with my red denim mini, I would have made scores. But there wasn't.

Religious as I was, my projects were always secular; my sister's were always profane. At one point it became her habit to paint obscenities in tidy cursive at the bottom of teacups she fashioned so carefully in ceramics class. You'd finish your Earl Grey only to find a polite request to go screw yourself. The saucer announced, "Suck it."

That was just fine with our mother. The main thing was that we were productive. Create, create, create. Every summer we filled the house with our crafty detritus, our braided rugs and hand-loomed pot holders, our colorful accessories spun from recycled rags. A pyramid of creations grew and grew on the designated arts and crafts table, or, as our mother called it, the "arts and craps table," because there was always so much shit on it.

"It looks like Colonial Williamsburg in here," our father would mutter, coming home from work and finding nowhere to place his briefcase but on a stack of hand-painted trivets.

He did not share our enthusiasm. Although he has a fine eye and a sure hand — I once came across a sketch of a crumpled napkin he'd drawn on a place mat while we waited for our food and was amazed by its sensitive detail — his interests lie elsewhere. He expresses himself creatively by rewiring the hi-fi components and packing the trunk for family trips.

Our father had reason to be wary of our crafts. He was often the victim of our artistic endeavors, the recipient of our misguided creations. For his birthday one year I made him a puffy pipe holder from quilt batting, cardboard, and calico. The end result was a cute 'n' cozy country craft that somehow managed to emasculate pipe-smoking, the most manly hobby in the world. My sister made him a hand-shaped ashtray whose fingers promptly broke off, leaving only the middle finger extended and whole. He was delighted, and it remained on the coffee table for weeks, offending all visitors, until it was finally relegated to a new home under the kitchen sink.

Although my father is such a conservative dresser he won't even wear jeans, we were undaunted. We provided him with a loud, ill-fitting wardrobe every year, subjecting him to garish ties, flamboyant hats, belly-baring vests that had turned out too short, floppy sweaters that had turned out too long. Sometimes the tastelessness was by accident and sometimes it was by design. It is a fact that my mother once spent months embroidering his surgical scrubs with a colorful R. Crumb–inspired panel that proudly proclaimed him "BORN TO BOOGIE" in big puffy letters. Even his own mother betrayed him, making him yarmulkes from crushed velvet and gold trim that resembled nothing so much as Victorian lamp shades.

Though he hates clutter, he is a sweet and sentimental man who never throws away anything his children have made for him. This is baggage for life, and we keep giving him more. As recently as last year, I made him a "fruit case": a hand-painted wooden box, lined in purple fun fur, designed to protect the pears he complains always get smashed when they go on picnics.

From time to time he tried to get us to tone things down, to slow the pace of production. When I was about five he became alarmed by the amount of fabric in the house — you could open a closet and be faced with a solid wall of gabardine — and asked my mother not to buy any more until she could make a dent in her back stock. She tried, but she couldn't always control herself. One of my earliest memories is of a trip my mother and sister and I made to San Francisco while my father was at a conference. We spent the entire day driving from one fabric store to the next. In between, my mother dashed into shops to buy us bribes — a doughnut, an ice-cream cone, a candy bar — quizzing us before she handed them over: "What are you going to tell Daddy we did today?" "We went to the museum." "Very good. Have a cruller." By the end of the day I was covered in eczema and vomiting into paper bags. This was the day we learned I was allergic to chocolate, and the day I learned to associate crafting with sweetness and excess.

We knew no restraints. Every summer witnessed a bumper crop of whatever craft had captivated us that particular year, our creations filling the house like so much zucchini. In 1981 we got caught in a cross-stitch frenzy and covered all available surfaces with our tiny x's. Another year it was needlepoint, and we churned out a variety of accoutrements, stitching over plastic canvas that could easily be made into cigarette cases, Bible covers, or, as we favored, simple wall hangings. Borrowing the popular catchphrase of the day, we needlepointed "Love is . . ." canvases for everyone we knew. "Love is Grandparents" went over big, but "Love is the Pool Guy" was met with bewilderment. Our efforts were further compromised by the fact that it was tricky to needle out legible letters and the recipients often couldn't read the mangled messages. "Low is the Hoonet"? the Hoovers asked. "Lay us the Hooker"?

We just didn't know when to stop, and our mother egged us on. "Don't let good taste hold you back," she urged. She always encouraged us toward the unsavory and the insipid, favoring fartsy over artsy. She herself once made my father an anatomically correct flasher doll from pantyhose stuffed with quilt batting, complete with a Brillo-topped crotch and a tiny trench coat. More recently she made a quilt that featured a little cabin amid some trees. When I remarked that it looked like Ted Kaczynski's shack, she was delighted and immediately embroidered "KEEP OUT. FBI, THIS MEANS YOU" on the cabin's front door.

We remain her protégés. We both went on to quasi careers in crafts, me writing craft books, my sister selling ceramics. Because I write for children, I try to keep it clean, but my sister has no such compunctions. She puts her art school education to good use making the line of "Shitbucket" teacups she feels compelled to produce. They sell remarkably well, but even if they didn't, she'd have to make them anyway. We were raised to believe that nothing is more important than giving outlet to our crassest artistic impulses. It informs everything we do. Even at her day job as a waitress, Vicky used to express herself much as she does with her ceramics, scrawling "Have a nice day, jerkoff!" inside customers' takeout containers. Well, we all have our missions.

In the Bible the big craftsman is Bezalel, whose name means "resting in the shade of the Divine," a fitting appellation for one so cool. I've always admired him, with his competence and easy assurance. We never hear about his self-doubts. "Are the acacia and gold leaf working together here?" "Do the purple and blue clash?" "Am I really good enough?" Moses asks that question all the time, but Bezalel just gets down to work. He's charged with the most important commission in human history and he just plows ahead, making the Ark of the Covenant as though he's assembling an entertainment center from IKEA, no sweat. By way of explanation we are told, simply, that he is "wise-hearted."

I'm just wise-assed. This is what happens when you learn to cross-stitch by making samplers that read "If Jackasses Could Fly, This Place Would Be an Airport." I never learned to play it straight. It's rare that I craft ritual objects, but when I do, they tend to be kitschy commentaries on the form, items like a Dr. Dre'dl or a Neil Tzedakah box.

For the most part I just don't make them at all. For me, crafting *is* the ritual. It's as comforting as reciting psalms, a meditative practice akin to prayer. It controls my tics and hushes my ruminations. It's secular but spiritual. I never feel as peaceful as I do when I'm elbow-deep in a project. And on those summer days, sitting on the air-conditioning vent while I needled out chestnuts like "We Don't Swim in Your Toilet . . ." I felt as contented as I ever could. Not like I was resting in the shade of the Divine, maybe, but pretty cool nonetheless.

FUN THINGS YOU CAN MAKE WITH KLEENEX

Think Kleenex is just for runny noses? Well, think again! It has more uses than duct tape. Versatile and sanitary, it's the crafter's miracle material. Here are some project ideas to get you started.

Hats
There's nothing like a new hat to pick you up when you're feeling down, or when you're feeling an overwhelming, mind-pricking need to cover your head in prayerful submission. So what do you do when you don't have a hat handy? Make one yourself! Simply unfold a Kleenex and place it on your head. Voilà! It's holy, hygienic, *and* high fashion. Wear it in the rain and you'll have instant papier-mâché — it's two crafts in one!

Gloves
Fingerless gloves are all the rage. Raging infection, that is. Lacy and insubstantial, they offer no protection against disease, and since they appeal to trashy girls who like to try them on even though they don't have enough cash to buy them, because they spent all their money on tattoos, yours probably came home from the store already loaded with germs. Toss your pair right in the garbage! You can craft a pristine replacement from your trusty Kleenex. Simply wrap Kleenex around your palm and you're done. Now you're sporting a trendy accessory that keeps disease at bay. The next time you need to open a door or shake a hand, line your palms with these handy helpers!

Seat Cushions

Seat cushions are a great project for the novice crafter. Just whip together a quick casing and slip it over a store-bought pillow form. In minutes, you've got a beautiful new cushion and a host of new contaminants — those pillow forms are just loaded! Forget the pillow form and craft your own by stuffing a Ziploc bag full of Kleenex. Cover with casing as usual. On second thought, why not skip the casing entirely? That fabric, I don't know, it just doesn't seem clean. The Ziploc bag, too. But what about the seat itself? That's definitely not clean. So let's just cover the seat with a fluffy nest of Kleenex. Sure, it's not as cushy as a nice tufted cushion, but what's more comfortable than knowing you're free from seat-borne contaminants?

Slippers

What to do when all the tissues get used up in a large-scale candusting emergency? Don't despair! The Kleenex may be gone, but the fun continues. Empty Kleenex boxes make a fine pair of shoes, favored by stylish jet-setters like Howard Hughes himself. Perfectly hygienic and orthopedic to boot (hah!), they'll protect your feet from contaminants like bacteria, feces, impure thoughts, and death.

Sunrise, Sunset: The Holidays

FOR THE BETTER part of my childhood, my Catholic mother was charged with my Jewish education. She was armed only with an LP of *Fiddler on the Roof* and a copy of *How to Be a Jewish Mother* a friend had given her as a joke. As a result, my early religious instruction consisted mostly of heavy sighs and gestures directed at the ceiling. "Such children I have," my mother prayed, lifting an open palm skyward. "Oy vey. The questions they ask."

Our questions were mostly about the holidays. The holidays are the sticking point of the interfaith family, the time at which differences are most noticeable and worrisome. We weren't particularly concerned about our immortal souls, but we did want to know if there would be presents and candy and a day off from school. My mother was straightforward and honest, answering our theological questions with admirable frankness: No, Santa

Claus didn't exist. The Easter Bunny was a fraud. And yes, the Tooth Fairy was totally, totally gay. A few years ago I found the stash of baby teeth and letters we'd exchanged for half-dollars over the years. Following my mother's instructions, we'd addressed our letters "Dear Bruce."

She was a good teacher. If we asked her a theological question she couldn't answer, she responded in philosophical Tevye fashion, "The sun rises, the sun sets. What are you going to do?"

The sun rises, the sun sets. It was more apt than my mother realized. This, in a phrase, was our family holiday experience. It was light and dark, good and bad, Catholic and Jewish, obsessive and compulsive. There were no matchmakers, no fiddlers, and no Cossacks, but vodka — there was a little of that.

WINTER

In December of 1974, the local newspaper ran a picture of my family trying to stuff a Christmas tree into our Volkswagen Beetle. There's my father, a Norman Rockwell figure with furrowed brow, pipe, and Coke-bottle glasses, struggling mightily with the tree while my mother and my sister and I, little Chers in ponchos and pigtails, look on with mild alarm. It was intended as a cute lifestyle photo, but as far as our family was concerned it was hard news. It was the first and last time we actually paid for a tree.

We weren't cheap so much as lazy. When you wait until December 24, no one's going to charge you for the crisp, teetering remains. Sometimes the lot let us have the tree for free. Other times we were given one by a school or a business already closed for the holiday. Usually we pulled a prematurely discarded tree off a neighbor's trash pile. One year we struck out entirely and had to decorate a houseplant instead, its tiny pathetic branches bending with the weight of a few tin ornaments. "A Christmas fern." My mother sighed. "It's the saddest, silliest thing I've ever seen in my life. It's a Christmas twee."

I'm not sure why we bothered with a tree at all. Decorating the tree was always an exercise in dysfunction, the occasion of our biggest annual family fight. My mother got annoyed because no one was doing enough to help; my sister and I sulked because my mother was yelling at us; and my father tried to look busy with some ancillary activity, mixing eggnog or adjusting the hi-fi to maximize the sound quality of the holiday sound track. We plowed through the job sullen and mute, shooting one another hostile looks as we piled on crocheted snowflakes, glitter-encrusted sugarplums, garish blinking lights, and a flurry of tinsel icicles. Being a family that refuses to throw anything away, we had hundreds of ornaments, half of them bent or broken but all of them still in play. We kept on decking until the tree was tarted up like a North Florida stripper. At that point we crowned the sagging mass with a fraying straw star: ta da, it was done. My mother stepped back to admire our work, swirling a glass of eggnog nearly brown with bourbon. "Well, that looks craptacular," she announced. "Happy Birthday, J. C."

It was always a disaster, a fire hazard, an eyesore. Even the family pets were moved to register their displeasure. The dog peed on it; the cat ate the needles. A tree doesn't belong in a house. More specifically, it didn't belong in *our* house. It was a violation of the promise the rabbi had extracted from my parents when he married them. Ours was to be a Jewish home, with Jewish kids:

no crucifixes, no crèches, a mezuzah on every doorpost, giant Stars of David clanging around all our necks. We would fly an Israeli flag from the front porch and on Sunday mornings we would gather, strong and tan from planting trees with our Zionist youth group, to toast our heritage as herring juice ran down our chins.

It was my father who broke the bargain and brought home the first tree when my sister and I were still babies. My mother was spending Christmas three thousand miles away from the rest of her family, with a husband who had to work Christmas Day and two children who were, likely as not, condemned to hell because she hadn't been permitted to baptize us. A tree was the least he could do. From there it all followed: the manger scene, the Advent calendar, the stuffed Santa, the silver angels, the red and green wooden block letters my sister always rearranged to spell S-A-T-A-N. A dinky menorah languished off to the side.

"The best of both worlds," family friends told us, clucking approvingly. "What lucky girls you are." But what did they know? Their families' biggest holiday dilemma was whipped or mashed; ours was only begotten son or false messiah. December is the hardest time of the year for an interfaith family. Oh sure, it sounds great: Maccabees and magi! Candles and carols! Festive meals and, best of all, the presents, double presents, eight days of Hanukkah plus Christmas, making nine glorious days of greed. But my friends' good-natured jealousy was sadly misplaced. The extra presents always turned out to be crap excavated from the bottom of my mother's purse, Kleenex packets and breath mints and ballpoint pens bearing Realtors' names. It's hard to sustain the holiday spirit of magic and miracles when you're staring down a stocking stuffed with disposable razors and key chains.

The interfaith feast that followed didn't make things any better. Latkes with ranch dressing and spiral-cut ham may be someone's idea of a dream dinner, but it sure wasn't mine.

I might have been a better sport if Hanukkah didn't get such short shrift. Hanukkah just can't compete. It was never supposed to. A minor holiday that got trumped up because of Christmas, it's like a cat in doll clothes, all trussed up in someone else's party dress and not very happy about it. But we try. Hanukkah is given its token treatment. In elementary school the duty fell to me. I was the only Jewish kid in all six grades. My teachers, flummoxed, always asked me to deliver the lesson. I dutifully prepared handouts and gave a presentation each year. It was only as an adult that I realized how I'd wasted the opportunity. My classmates knew nothing about Judaism; I could have made everything up. "On Hanukkah, Jews are given high-ticket gifts by their gentile friends, who receive nothing in return. On the first night, the Jews are gifted with hair appliances such as curling irons and diffusers. The second night, it is traditional to give consumer electronics, portable stereos and the like. The third night is for gourmet luxuries like aged steaks. Throughout the whole eight days it is customary for gentiles to offer Jews the choicest selections from their lunches and to do the Jews' homework."

My classmates would have fallen for it. I was the only Jew any of them knew, and they tended to overcompensate trying to prove they didn't hold my faith against me. After we first learned about the Holocaust, in fourth grade, a classmate approached me, her eyes wet. "I'm one-eighth German and I feel just awful for what my people did to your people," she confessed. "Please accept this gum as a token of apology."

Yes, I thought. Bring me your reparations. All of you who've never received a mezuzah for Christmas, who aren't crossed by crosses and stars, come before me and present your tribute. Bring your Juicy Fruit and your fruit roll-ups, your candy canes and your chocolate coins, all of it, anything to sweeten the taste in my mouth.

Nine years old and I was already as bitter as the green cherries dotting the Christmas stollen. By the time I was in high school I'd cast myself as the Little Match Girl in our domestic holiday drama, a world-class sulker hosting a pity party of epic proportions. I was furious that we made so little fuss over Hanukkah and so much over Christmas, furious that we were marking Christmas at all. I mourned missing out on the December 25th experience a Jew is supposed to have, eating Chinese food, renting movies, and making obscene amounts of overtime pay at work. Come Christmas morning I refused to get excited about even the good gifts, preferring to spend the day in a holiday snit. Why should I have to celebrate Christmas? This wasn't part of the deal, we were supposed to be raised Jewish, no Christianity in the home, it's not fair, this sucks, this *sucks*, and that brand-new Atari is making it suck only a tiny bit less.

My mother is too well-adjusted for self-pity, but I know those holidays were no fiesta for her, either. She had to deal with my fits while quietly suppressing her own. A devout Catholic, she's spent the last thirty years celebrating Christmas with three people who acknowledge the birthday boy only by taking his name in vain. Watching her trudge off to midnight mass by herself always broke my heart, though never enough to make me join her, as that would have meant missing the late-night dating shows I enjoyed so much. But maybe I should have. She deserves that. She deserves the tree, the trimmings, all of it. This holiday business isn't her fault; it isn't anybody's fault. Even if my father hadn't caved that first Christmas, the fall was bound to come. Who can resist Christmas? It's Christmas! Even my Jewish relatives decorate their homes with green lights and red bows.

In college I tried to flee it, went to the most Jewish places I could think of, Jerusalem or Miami, where December 25 was just another day. No carols, no candy canes — it was what I'd wanted all my life. But it wasn't how I'd pictured it at all. I'd imagined myself watching the sunset on a Tel Aviv beach as my swarthy escort brought me ouzo after ouzo, forgetting the holiday entirely until I noticed the date on my *Herald Tribune.*

Instead I found myself looking for the nearest Santa, so desperate I would have sat in the lap of any fat guy in a red tracksuit. I missed my family and I missed the festivity. One Christmas Eve in Israel I was so homesick I went to Bethlehem. But it wasn't like home at all. At home I don't get my inner thighs patted down by enthusiastic soldiers, and even if I did, it wouldn't be the highlight of my day. What a sad, sorry, inauspicious Christmas that was. The Gulf War was just a few weeks away, and few pilgrims were bold enough to brave the impending invasion of Scud missiles and CNN reporters. Manger Square was bare of any decorations save a lone, tired tinsel garland. The only visitors were a motley, disoriented, and sedated-looking choir of Korean Baptists swaying unsteadily on a set of rickety bleachers, singing off-key carols in heavily accented English, their only audience a roving band of local children aggressively selling stale wafer cookies.

There were no magi in Bethlehem that day. But I did leave there wiser. I resolved that that would be the last holiday season I would spend away from my family, and it was. From then on I would embrace it as an opportunity to cherish my family, and my family would cherish me right back. This probably had less to do with any profound epiphany than with the fact that by the next Christmas I was of legal drinking age. We learned that the best way to get into the holiday spirit is with some holiday spirits. Now my father gets the day off to a good start by packing our muskets with cocktails at eleven a.m., and it's smiles all day. Happy holidays, everybody. Happy holidays, indeed.

SPRING

It has always puzzled me that so many cultures have a springtime interval of asceticism and mourning. Catholics have Lent; Jews have the Omer; Pentecostals have the end of squirrel-hunting season. It seems contrary to human nature to mortify the flesh just when it's getting warm enough to bare it. But perhaps that's why these periods of subdued brooding are necessary. With all the bees buzzing and blossoms blooming, surely we'd be leaping into orgies and binges if our faiths didn't require us to abstain, reflect, postpone joy.

In our house there was little risk of anyone dying of happiness in the spring. The interfaith confluence of holidays guaranteed this was the worst eating we would do all year. We were crippled not only by Passover's prohibition on leaven but by Lent's prohibition on meat. Also out was whatever staple food my mother had decided to give up, usually chocolate or ice cream. As bad as this was, it didn't approach the unhappiness my cousin caused when he gave up sarcasm for Lent; he offended his friends for six full weeks, all of them so used to his tongue-in-cheek comments that they didn't realize that by "Nice haircut," he really meant "Nice haircut."

But for the rest of us sarcasm was sustenance, the manna that got us through the miserable stretch of meals. *"Delicious dinner." "Great omelet. I never would have thought of mixing in sardines! It's fantastic." "I wish we could eat matzo and scrod all year round."* We were cranky and crampy. Protein and matzo are constipating enough taken alone, but consumed together they form a compound that will obstruct the bowel for weeks on end. I find it no small irony that we celebrate the Festival of Freedom by eating a food that's so very binding. Let my people go, indeed. In our house, the holiday was known as Gassover.

One year the cat joined us in protest by appropriating the holy palm my mother had brought home from church. For an entire week he carried it around in his mouth like a big green Fu Manchu mustache, his fanged overbite making him look both dippy and pissed off. That year the parish priest had given a particularly strident speech about the importance of respecting the palm, and my mother was appalled. But there was no getting it back. When we tried to confiscate it, he either found where we'd hidden it or whined until we produced it. "Do you think that's bad for him?" my father asked. "Well, it being a *sin*, yeah, I'd say it's pretty bad for him," my mother replied. "Let's hope there's no cat hell."

Or let's hope there is; surely that's the one place there's no fish. My least favorite food, it appeared in every course when seder and Good Friday coincided. The main event was always an old Lenten family recipe called "Fancy Fish," which consisted of sole dredged in mayonnaise and topped with bread crumbs, here replaced by matzo meal. Bad as it was, at least it knew its place; at least it didn't try to be a dessert. Gefilte fish does. Gefilte fish is the Spam of the Jewish people. It is our national culinary disgrace. We eat it because it never occurs to us that we don't have to. It tastes like cat food, but even our cat wouldn't eat it. It is a nugget of carp-flavored cement, a clot of ashen misery. It is the color of despair, almost funerary, musty and sweet. Sweeter still was our seder wine, a screw-top kosher affair that promised notes of Marshmallow Fluff. "The label says it's 'cream finish'" my father would say with a smile, filling our glasses. "I think we're in for a treat."

The next day we reeled from the sulfite headaches, but what could we do? We were lucky to get what we got. There weren't more than ten Jewish families in our hometown, so there was almost nothing available. We had to drive to the next town over just to get matzo. Our local supermarket tried, though, bless their hearts, running an ad for Passover specials that featured clip art of a glass of wine, a loaf of bread, and a cross. They got the artwork wrong, but at least the timing was right. The Hanukkah specials were offered a full two weeks after Hanukkah ended and consisted, inexplicably, of egg noodles and "Congratulations on Your Bar Mitzvah" cards.

Between the bad food and the approaching bikini season, Passover was prime time for my biannual flare-up of anorexia. On the alternate years, the scrupulosity kicked in. Passover is high season for the disorder. It's the only holiday that actually demands a comprehensive hosing-down of the house and all its contents, a requirement that flipped all my scrupulous switches. Even sane people go nuts on Passover. The holiday compels perfectly normal adults to board the pets, bleach the phones, and cover all the countertops with foil. On Passover, everyone's kitchen looks like a bad sci-fi movie set. The scrupulous take the process into another realm altogether. No amount of foil or cleaning will suffice. For the scrupulous, it's Passoverandoverandoveragain.

To make matters worse, there's no room for error as there is with other commandments. You're not to mix meat and milk, you're to take every precaution, but if there's the slightest contamination, it's still kosher. Not so with Passover. Any amount of leaven renders everything it touches unfit. Leaven is a huge category to begin with, consisting not just of bread and baked goods but of all legumes, all grains, and all their derivatives, including wonderful additives like MSG. There is leaven in ketchup, in salsa, in soda, powdered sugar, pickles, shampoo. I often think how much easier our lives might be if, in their haste to leave Egypt, the Israelites had skipped the unleavened loaves altogether and had just packed, say, some underripe fruit. If we were to observe Passover with limits on produce instead of leaven, it would be a much simpler affair. Fruit is large, easy to spot, and doesn't produce crumbs. For a week we'd have to have honey instead of jam with our peanut butter. Big deal.

But leaven, leaven is hard. And I made it much harder. In my bursts of scrupulosity I extrapolated leaven to include not just food but words and pictures. The issue of *Woman's Day* with the cake on the cover had to be sealed away with the rest of the contraband under the bathroom sink. If I accidentally glanced at the still life of bread and grapes, I had to go wash and chant and pray.

Books were out; two or three pages in, a character would have lunch, the word *sandwich* would get on my hands, and I'd be contaminated. TV was impossible, with all the ads for tacos and snack cakes. It would have been an unbearably boring time if I hadn't been so busy flushing my mouth out and inspecting the dog's fur for crumbs.

Perhaps it would have been easier if I'd had any idea what I was doing. Mr. Stein and I hadn't covered the holidays yet. My knowledge of Passover customs was limited to what I'd picked up from a few half-baked seders and the annual hippie Passover potluck in the nearby college town, attended mostly by bearded grad students wearing T-shirts proclaiming "I'm a *real* man now that I've got matzo balls." Educational, but not in the way one might hope.

I didn't know what I was doing at all. I didn't know you were actually supposed to have a seder on both the first and second nights until I was twelve. I was horrified. My family only did the one. And so began my custom of conducting the second seder secretly in my room, in the dark, while the rest of the family was downstairs watching TV. It was lonely and weird, with me reading all the responses and pantomiming the food, but it was oddly satisfying, too. My family wasn't there to mess things up, and with the beginnings of a bowel impaction rumbling in my colon, the invisible food was a relief.

It was a shadowy phantom service that in its strange, bleak way perfectly embodied the subdued mood of the season, the gathering darkness of a profound depression that waited for me, a ways off but already inevitable. It grew closer and closer as I bent over my Haggadah, an ancient battered relic illustrated with stark

Munch-style woodcuts of the Angel of Death and suffering Egyptians. Years before, the dog had gotten ahold of it and his bite marks only added to the gruesome specter. It was perfect. Hours later, after I finally finished and went to bed, I dreamed of dog-faced pharaohs chasing me with enema hoses, as my hands framed an O-shaped silent scream. "Let my people go," I tried to yell, but nothing, nothing would come out.

SUMMER

Summer may be the simplest time of the year for an interfaith family, simply because there are so few holidays to cause conflict. For a family with an obsessive-compulsive child, however, it's ninety days of unremitting hell. Your kid is home twenty-four hours a day, with nothing to distract her but her own wacked-out preoccupations.

In our house, of course, we had all the handicrafts. This turned out to be a trade-off. It helped keep my obsessions and compulsions in check, but not my bad taste. Every summer I produced a series of terrifically unappealing knitted vests and neckties that were no less annoying than constant washing and reassurance-seeking. Perhaps my mother should have encouraged me to take up smoking instead.

Whatever my new hobby, it would all grind to a halt in early July, with the arrival of the Three Weeks. The Three Weeks is a period of mourning for the destruction of the Temple during which anything of interest is prohibited. Knitting, shopping, interior decorating — all of these things are out. It is forbidden to get a haircut or blow out candles, to dance or play music, to sew or shave or wear new clothes. During the last nine days there are even more restrictions: no eating meat, no drinking wine, no swimming, washing, laundering, or bathing. On the last day, the fast of Tisha b'Av, the prohibitions increase: one may not eat or drink, nor, more strangely, may one wear leather or moisturize. Given the prohibitions on booze and hygiene, it goes without saying that there is also no fooling around.

As fun as the Three Weeks are, it's hard to believe they're not more widely observed. Most Jews haven't even heard of them. My interfaith family certainly hadn't, and they didn't quite know what to make of it when I first introduced the concept. "Let me get this straight," my mother puzzled. "For the next three weeks you're not going to rearrange my furniture, play your klezmer tape, or shave your armpits?" I was shocked when she announced that was just fine with her. My family had learned to question and then forbid anything I insisted was a commandment, but they let this one go. I'd made up some weird stuff, sure, but even I wasn't this arbitrarily masochistic. In any case, it seemed like an even trade. My family would have to put up with my BO and the scratch marks my stubble left on the leather couch, but they would finally get a turn in the shower.

During my scrupulous periods the Three Weeks were both exquisitely satisfying and impossible. I loved the additional restrictions, the new list of pleasures denied, but the ban on washing, oh, the ban on washing. Washing normally occupied a good two hours of my day. Forced to give up my favorite hobby, I was bored witless. I also stank. I am not an active person, but nine days without a bath will sour the cream of any couch potato. I would later learn that my observance was a little overzealous —

the ban on shaving applies only to men, and the ban on washing is observed largely in the breach — but at the time I could do nothing but stew in my own natural juices.

It was in this matted and fragrant condition that I celebrated my late-July birthday. When my family sang the "Happy Birthday" variant, "You look like a monkey, and you smell like one, too," they weren't teasing so much as reporting the sad truth. It's a horrible time for any observant Jew to have a birthday, but for a scrupulous one, it's particularly unpleasant. I took all the Three Weeks customs to the extreme. My zealous unhappiness is well-documented in all my teenage birthday photos, year after year the same picture: a greasy me, grimacing in front of a cake I'm going to make an excuse not to eat, topped by candles I'm going to fake an asthma attack not to blow out. Out of frame is the odd assortment of gifts I've requested. Because I can't accept clothes or music, I will get Jewish encyclopedias, playing cards, stationery, and novelty Band-Aids.

When I turned eighteen my birthday fell on Tisha b'Av itself. Normally I was not permitted to observe it, but as I was now an adult responsible for screwing up my own life, my parents let me fast. "Me, I'd be out buying lotto tickets and porn, but if you want to celebrate your eighteenth birthday working up a good faint, knock yourself out," my mother said, returning the cake mix to the pantry.

The number eighteen is hugely significant in Judaism, and if I'd been a counter I probably would have spent all day trying to determine the auspiciousness of this coincidence. But since I was a washer, I had nothing at all to do. It is amazing how much free time you have when you're not permitted to eat or groom. After spending a few hours trying to catalog the family snapshots, I grew bored and wandered next door to see our only Jewish neighbors. Their teenage niece was visiting from Tel Aviv. It was 110 degrees, and she was in the backyard, splashing in the pool. I was covered wrist to ankle in corduroy. Michal took one look at me and rolled her eyes. "Come in," she offered. "You will be really more comfortable in the waters."

I explained that I couldn't because it was Tisha b'Av. "I know what is Tisha b'Av," she replied, giving me a withering look that suggested it was people like me who'd driven her from Israel to California in the first place. "You speak Hebrew? You know what is *meshuga?*"

She was the only person I'd met who'd actually heard of this holiday and even she thought I was nuts. I suppose I should have been offended, but I was charmed. Here was that Israeli candor I'd heard so much about. It was as refreshing and tart as a glass of lemonade. Who needed a dip in the pool when the conversation was this bracing?

I smiled at her dumbly, like a dog that wags its tail when you curse it in a dulcet tone. Michal swam over to the edge. "Well, then, I think we must to go inside, before you fall from the heat weakness." She sighed, lifting herself out of the pool. "I know something we can do that is okay with Torah and not too boring."

We spent the rest of the afternoon poring over back issues of the Hebrew equivalent of *Cosmo*. Oh, sure, with all the cleavage and sex tips, it was not the most appropriate reading material for the blackest day of Jewish history. Under other circumstances I might have balked, but I was afraid to argue with Michal. Besides, it was a wonderful opportunity to expand my knowledge of the holy tongue. We leafed through page by page, lying on our stomachs in the dark, cool guest room, discussing the pictures while she translated the articles for me. "This one is about a woman who, em, I'm not sure how you say, she is not liking the size of her chests."

I learned all kinds of important words that day, the Hebrew terms for *exfoliate, mousse, cellulite,* and *chafing.* And while I picked up plenty of important information about dressing to suit your body type, the most significant lesson I learned was a sociological one. I'd expected Israel to be populated by tanner but equally religious clones of myself. Michal's magazines revealed that it was populated by Miss Teen Universe hopefuls. These weren't the people of the book, but of the *Redbook.* I should have been disappointed, shocked, but instead I was exhilarated. It had never occurred to me that you could have both faith and flesh, that, like the pool, you could be both deep and shallow at once.

In a strange way, it was an appropriate lesson. Fast days have different jobs. Yom Kippur is meant to take one out of one's body. But Tisha b'Av is meant to place one firmly in it, as hot and dirty and weak as it may be. I don't think it was just coincidence that a few weeks later I began to trade ascetic for aesthetic, doing things I hadn't done since the anorexia and scrupulosity first hit: conditioning my hair, wearing perfume, eating an eclair. A few weeks after that I would start college and begin, for the first time in years, to live a normal life.

My brain was finally doing what it was supposed to. It would be quite some time before my hair would, too.

FALL

Fall may be the best time of the year for Jews. The cool, dry weather is easy on frizz, and it's high season for the only competitive sport we care for, shopping wholesale. With all the High Holidays, there are plenty of occasions to model our fall fashions, and on one of them we're actually *commanded* to wear new clothes. My family usually managed a trip to Loehmann's, but the rest of our High Holiday observance tended to be rather erratic. For instance, we normally failed to go to synagogue. When we did go, we spent most of the service commenting on others' outfits. "Check out the lady in the back," we whispered. "Can she really think it's a good idea to wear patterned hose on the day we're asked to account for our sins?" In this, if in nothing else, we marked the holiday as we're intended to. If Jews weren't supposed to spend the High Holidays criticizing one another's clothes we would have been born Mormons.

We usually managed a festive dinner, even when it wasn't entirely appropriate. On more than one Yom Kippur, we marked the occasion by having a big dinner out. On more than one Yom Kippur, the menu included pork. Our other customs were similarly off, informed less by religious sensibility than an interfaith multicultural flair for entertaining. Once, my mother brought home a Rosh Hashana piñata. "It's festive," she explained. "And we might feel like hitting something later." My father's family, Russian by way of Shanghai, contributed piroshki and red envelopes of lucky New Year money. I was in college before I learned this was a Chinese custom and not a Jewish one.

To my friends, it was all foreign anyway. "Happy Rosh Man-ana!" they wished me. There were too many holidays, all with funny names; who could keep them straight? They could never remember which was the festive new-year one and which was the somber fasting one. "Have a super-fun holiday," they urged me the day before Yom Kippur. "Don't eat too much of that kegel!" One year, while I was home fasting, a friend dropped by bearing a steaming white box. "It's a Yom Kippur pizza," he explained. "I don't know how your people celebrate, but this is what my folk always eat on holidays." Apparently his folk weren't concerned with cholesterol or kashrut; it was a sausage-pepperoni combo.

My friends were confused by the whole High Holiday pro-duction, but they understood one thing: I got to stay home from school, and this was to be envied. Every fall my classmates pelted me with questions about conversion. "What if you've already been circumcised?" they asked. "Are you good to go?"

I answered their questions politely, but inside I scoffed at their ignorance. They had *no idea*. My days off were hard-won in annual pitched battles with my parents. The outcome was always the same: I was permitted Yom Kippur and one day of Rosh Hashana, but I was nuts if I thought I was getting off for Sukkot. "Suck what?" my family asked. "You made that one up."

I knew better than to ask for Shemini Atzeret and Simchat Torah. Even *I* thought they sounded fake. But they're holy days all. Be they Reform, Conservative, or Orthodox, practicing Jews take these days off, but my parents refused to believe me. Every year, they made me spend those days fuming in a classroom. I was furious, but I could hardly blame them. Right or wrong, I always argued my point with equal fervor. I had insisted just as stridently that I needed to procure some hyssop to cleanse the ritual impurity I had incurred by swimming in a public pool. How were they to distinguish between two practices that looked equally crazy? I was going to school, and that was that.

Going to class on holidays was an agonizing ordeal. Every word I had to write, every number I had to calculate — each violation of the holy day was torturous, a bamboo shoot under a nail. But I was determined to get at least partial credit for observing the holiday, and that meant doing the absolute minimum of schoolwork. The point was to do as little as I possibly could without earning detention, where, I was sure, I would be required to violate the holiday in some other way, cleaning blackboards or helping the loadies heat their freebase. When I had to write, I used short words and abbreviations; one less letter meant one less sin. I pretended not to know answers, feigned hand cramps and headaches, anything to avoid participation. For an unrepentant know-it-all like me, playing dumb was abject misery. Ultimately, though, it was a very satisfying arrangement, one that killed two birds with one stone: by shirking the work, I managed to both avoid violating the holiday and punish myself for coming to school in the first place. Asked to diagram an independent clause on the board, I puzzled my classmates and embarrassed myself with a succinct gem like "I no good now; food make sick." It was thirty-three letters shorter than "I am nauseous today; the Russian fish pastries did not agree with me."

It didn't seem fair. Here, finally, were holidays that weren't competing with more exciting Christian festivals and still my interfaith family was getting in the way. School was the least of it.

My parents and my sister all have birthdays that fall within a three-week period in midautumn; invariably, they are on the High Holidays. My sister's sixteenth birthday landed square on Yom Kippur. I had hoped to spend the evening at synagogue, fasting, light as an angel in a white dress, swaying with shut eyes as the plaintive melody of the Kol Nidre transported me to a higher dimension. Instead I had to accompany the rest of the family to the restaurant my sister chose, a sprawling, kitsch-laden, brass-fixtured establishment named Bobby McGee's. It was favored by prom-goers and young singles, who loved its Top-40 DJ and menu of pizzajitas and deep-fried finger foods. The restaurant's signature was the commemorative keepsake ceramic cups its cocktails came in. You could drink your piña colada out of a lady's boot, a bathtub, or, best of all, a toilet.

I spent the entire night sulking in a drop-waisted dress six years too young for me and picking at my steamed vegetable plate. "What's the matter, Jen?" my family inquired, shouting over the "woo-hoos!" of our fellow diners. "Buck up. Come on. Have another toilet full of virgin strawberry daiquiri."

I wanted to go off to the bathroom to fume in peace or maybe to pray in a stall, but that meant crossing the *Saturday Night Fever*–style neon checkerboard dance floor. It was crowded with singles in synthetic fibers who wouldn't move out of the way for a seventeen-year-old girl in enormous glasses dressed like Rebecca of Sunnybrook Farm. I remained at the table, gripping my toilet and thinking such horrible thoughts that I would have plenty to atone for the next morning.

That was the last Yom Kippur I would spend with my family for fifteen years. Between the disinterest and the pork, I thought I was better off celebrating the High Holidays alone. We would re-solve the Christmas conflict and the Passover problems, but the crutches that got us through those times — a.m. drinking and bitter sarcasm — felt out of place on the holiest of days. My par-ents would call me to wish me a *goot yontiff,* and I would keep my distance, and this seemed to work out very well for everyone.

But fifteen years have passed since my religiosity made my family want to smother me, fifteen years since their flippancy made me want to stone them. Now even my father fasts on Yom Kippur, though he insists he does it only for the weight-loss ben-efits. Ever so slowly, we are inching toward a détente.

The High Holidays are about tradition, but they're also about reconciliation. I've reconciled to my interfaith lot, even grown to appreciate it. It was in this spirit of reconciliation that I recently invited my parents to join me for our first Rosh Hashana together in many years. The theme was perfect, reflecting my Jewish heritage, my rural upbringing, and my shikse roots: Rosh HaShania, a tribute to country-western darling Shania Twain. Over Little Debbies and cheap red wine, we wished for a good and sweet new year. It was.

CULTURALLY INAPPROPRIATE GIFTS I HAVE RECEIVED FROM SANTA CLAUS

1. Two albums of Hasidic folk songs
2. The collected works of Isaac Bashevis Singer
3. The collected works of Saul Bellow
4. The collected works of Chaim Potok
5. Jewish engagement calendar (yearly, 1981–1992)
6. Coffee-table book on Jewish art
7. Anthology of Jewish poetry
8. Menorah and handmade candles
9. Mezuzah
10. Hanukkah-themed socks

All Is Vanity

W HEN I WAS four and my sister was three, our parents enrolled us in the Lutheran preschool favored by our neighbors.
Normally I get nervous when I am surrounded by autoharp-
playing Christians, but we liked it there. It was a cheerful place
run by friendly, affectionate grandmothers. If our parents were
worried about us picking up any Protestant traits like, say, a work
ethic, their fears were put to rest when we failed to complete any
assignments besides Snack and Nap. The scant religious instruction they offered was of a nonsectarian feel-good stripe, a Care
Bear belief system that taught us to share and recycle.

It was there that I learned to pray. Prayer was like a phone call
to heaven, our teachers told us. You could say thanks, or you
could ask for something very important, like peace and happiness. We knelt in a circle and one by one we said our prayers out

loud. Some children prayed for an end to hunger. Others prayed for all the sick babies in the world. I prayed for makeup.

Had I been pressed, I might have explained that I simply wanted to make the world a more beautiful place. What I really wanted was a little sparkle. At four, it was already very apparent to me that I had the kind of features that required some extra help. Four was an awkward age for me. I hadn't quite worked out a wardrobe strategy and I'd been given a regrettable short haircut that frequently got me mistaken for a boy. Nothing would put a stop to that quicker than a nice smart lipstick, I thought.

Prayer was the only way I was going to get it. My mother refused to buy me makeup, a position I found completely unreasonable. Why shouldn't a preschooler wear a little lip color and mascara? I was just trying to work with what I had.

My mother had been intractable, but now here was this wonderful thing called prayer. Here was a force that could overrule her. I began making fervent entreaties each night before bed. "When I wake up please let there be rose frost lipstick, powder blusher, and cream eye shadow in sea foam green on my bedside table," I prayed. "If it will make it easier for You I can mark the pages in the Avon catalog. Thank You very much."

Three weeks later my mother produced a yellow plastic compact shaped like a baby chick, which opened to reveal a mirror and a tin of solid perfume. I was captivated. Sure, it wasn't really makeup. It was colorless and did nothing for my thin upper lip or patchy eyebrows. I didn't care. It smelled wonderful. It was good enough.

And it had come to me through prayer, thereby forever cementing the link between cosmology and cosmetology in my

brain. From that moment on, like many women of deep faith —
Tammy Faye Baker, Mary Kay Ash, Anita Bryant — I believed a
spiritual life demanded the liberal and constant use of cosmetics
and accessories. I worshipped all the trappings of womanhood:
jewelry, makeup, purses, and panty hose. These things were holy.
They were prim and pure. They were also immensely satisfying
to my obsessive-compulsive mind. The way I saw it, they kept
your hands and mind busy, giving you something to retouch,
smooth, adjust, and pluck out of crevices. Sure, it was compulsive
behavior, but it was compulsive behavior that paid off in the form
of a more attractive self.

My other compulsive habits did not necessarily do this. I had
some grooming compulsions, but they did not leave me looking
particularly well-groomed. There was, for instance, the trichotillo-
mania, the urge to pull out hair. Of all obsessive-compulsives,
trichotillomaniacs are the easiest to spot, because they're the ones
without any eyebrows. My case was mild and occasional, but every
once in a while, I was overwhelmed. Hairs demanded to be pulled,
skin to be picked. A little bare patch here, an infected sore there —
it was nothing you'd notice, not if properly concealed with the
foundation and hairpieces I begged my mother to buy.

These were not attractive habits. Less attractive still was the
constant compulsion to pick my nose. I knew how bad it looked,
but I just couldn't keep my finger out of my nostril. "That's our
little miner," my mother commented, when strangers looked on
in horror. "We think she has a real future as a garbage picker.
When she's old enough we're going to send her to Rio to teach
those Brazilian street kids a thing or two."

My mother joked about it, but it bothered her, and she did what she could to get me to stop. "Digging for gold again, I see," she would sigh, driving the car, as I looked out the window and rooted absently around in a nostril. "Well, you can pan that stream all you want, but it's never going to pay off."

I ignored the flip comments, but the bribe got my attention. If I could keep my fingers holstered and my nose loaded for a month, my mother promised, I would get a ring and bracelet set. I was helpless before shiny, girly trinkets, and my mother won. Soon my finger was adorned with a tiny faux emerald that I had not, for once, harvested myself.

My mother had discovered my Achilles' heel, and it was a strappy open-toed little number. But I'd sold out too cheap. The ring and bracelet set was all I was going to get, and after the perfume compact, the makeup pipeline dried up, too. My mother did, however, permit me a purse and some low-heeled mules. I took to shuffling behind her on her errands, stuffing my pocketbook with anything that was free: brochures on high blood pressure, samples of hand lotion, Sweet'n Low packets, Kleenex, and aluminum ashtrays. "It's like shopping with Great-Aunty Mee-Maw," my mother muttered. Hardly, I thought. Great-aunties, at least, were allowed blush.

I got nothing. I was really hoping for some frilly lingerie. Here, too, my mother was intractable. Exactly what is so disturbing about a four-year-old wearing a French-cut matching bra and panty set? I wanted to know. Once again I was forced to rely on my own resourcefulness. After I saw a picture of a flapper wearing a garter, I tried to fashion one for myself by putting a ponytail elastic around my thigh. It had a one-inch diameter. By the time my mother noticed what I'd done, my leg was maroon.

One afternoon I found my mother crying in her bedroom. Her brother had died in a boating accident, and she had just received the telegram telling her his body had been found. I didn't fully understand what had happened, but I knew I'd never seen her so upset. What could I say to help her put things in perspective, to remind her that the circle of life goes on? What I came up with was this: "Mom, when you die, can I have your bras?"

I considered good foundation garments a matter of the most solemn importance, so it seemed an appropriate response. In retrospect, I think it was a little callous. In any case, it was ineffectual. Even if she did leave me the good Maidenforms, I knew it would be decades before I got my hands on them. My mother appeared to be in excellent health. And she was unlikely to hand them over in a burst of madcap exuberance. This was not a happy time. My mother's father had died just a year before, her mother, ten years before that, making my mother an orphan at thirty-two. Across the street, Mrs. Foster was dying a slow and painful death from liver cancer that turned her eyes and skin a deep canary, and it was my mother's unhappy volunteer project to give her daily sponge baths. Mrs. Foster died within a year, living just long enough to bury her two-year-old daughter, who died after consuming a bottle of her mother's medication.

I remember this as a dark, uneasy period, steeped in '70s earth tones that flattered none of us; we are a sallow family. The earth tones, I'm sure, contributed to our general malaise. And in a deeper way, those yellows and rusts came to represent the subdued, jaundiced time. This was our blue period, painted in sickly shades of ochre and carbuncle.

At four, I didn't fully understand everything that was going on, but the frailty of the body, I got. This I understood. Bodies could break. They broke all the time. They had to be controlled, groomed, tricked up with embellishments to hide their failings. They had to be painted and plucked. That's all we had to protect us, these cosmetics and compulsions. All we could do was put some makeup on the bruise, count all our arm hairs, and move on. So I ticced and tapped and tweezed. You work with what you have.

And it succeeded; things improved. Family members and neighbors stopped dying. The earth tones of the '70s gave way to the purples and teals of the '80s. We began to feel happy and safe. When things got better my compulsions waned, but my interest in makeup did not. By age eight I was making my own cosmetic preparations, all of them consisting of nothing but my own saliva. I licked my lips constantly to impart a moist, glossy sheen. I wet my eyelashes to mimic mascara, my brows to approximate brow pencil. My face was continually basted in my own spit. It left my skin chapped and the upholstery soiled, but what could I do? I was forced to turn to the resources of my own body. Failing blush, I chewed my cheeks raw sucking in and biting down to create the impression of cheekbones.

"What's with that face?" my mother asked.

Speaking would have required me to release the clamp I had on my cheeks, so I responded by arching a brow and mimicking a face I'd seen Cybill Shepherd make.

"I'm not sure what you're doing, but that's not a face you want to make at your mother. Cut it out."

Finally my mother broke down. She agreed to let me have some cosmetics as long as she didn't have to pay for them and I promised not to wear them outside. I spent my allowance on maraschino-bright used lipsticks I found at garage sales. "Doesn't look septic to me!" she announced cheerfully, unworried that the expiration date was twenty years past. When I was nine she thought me old enough for her own cast-off cosmetics and happily handed over her tangerine lipsticks and magenta eye shadow. "Look at you!" she exclaimed the first time I came to dinner made up like a showgirl in shades of flame-retardant Vegas carpet. "I think that's a special look just for tonight, okay?"

The next day my eyes and mouth were ringed with an angry rash, but I was undaunted. I was allergic to expired cosmetics, apparently, but that didn't mean I had to go without. I could make my own all-natural products. I promptly concocted a signature scent from beheaded marigolds pickled in dishwashing liquid and my mother's Jean Naté. It was a mixed success. I liked the scent just fine, but at dinner that night my father demanded to know who smelled like compost, and the bee stings dotting my face made the culprit easy to track down.

Still, I was not discouraged. My next creation was an all-purpose preparation I called "Beauty Sauce." It was a blend of lotion, bubble bath, shampoo, conditioner, solid perfume, beer, and pancake syrup, mixed together in a peanut butter jar. It immediately thickened and grew mold. At a loss, I hid it under the bathroom sink, where it remained until I went to college.

Shortly after that experiment my affection for cosmetics

soured, too. Adolescence began, and my relationship with cosmetics, like my relationships with good humor and common sense, became an on-again, off-again affair. I had never expected this, but there it was. Now that I was finally old enough to wear makeup outside the house, I found that I didn't want to. Sometimes I couldn't because the scrupulosity forbade it; other times, because good taste did. I was in junior high now, but I was very short, and the least bit of makeup made me look like a pageant baby.

My sister had no such reservations. By now she, too, had discovered makeup, and her typical preteen bungling of the medium did little to reignite my interest. She favored attention-getting colors and circled her features in liner, making her face look like it had undergone a particularly thorough copyedit. She came to the breakfast table furry with powder and foundation, not managing to even get a lipstick print on her juice glass before my parents marched her back upstairs to tone it down. When they slept in on weekends, she snuck out with a full face on, the application so heavy-handed that even strangers were moved to offer advice.

"My niece has your coloring, and we found that fawn eye shadow suits her much better than the navy blue you've got on there," a saleslady told her. "Some people think you have to *choose* between a bright blusher and a bright lipstick, and experience has taught us that's a good rule to follow."

The same saleslady scanned my washed-out features and asked if I was sick, but I figured too little was better than too much. I was having none of this. It was tacky and immodest. It was idolatrous and treyf. Later I would meet yeshiva girls and learn that even drag queens don't wear as much mascara, but at the time I thought cosmetics were unkosher. Lip balm, soap, shampoo, deodorant: all these things were out. The multipurpose saliva I had relied on as an eight-year-old was out, too. Who knew where my mouth had been?

But then the scrupulosity would subside, the skies would clear, and I'd find myself ankle-deep in a paraffin bath. The energy I put into inspecting the carpets during my scrupulous periods went into pore wrangling during my sane ones. I spent my babysitting money on Ten-O-Six and department store moisturizers. I formed friendships with the offspring of Amway sales reps, helping myself to the free samples of night cream they kept around the house.

On weekends I turned the kitchen into my own personal day spa, making messy, complicated treatments from the family's lunch fixings. "This is so unsanitary," my mother complained when I took up residence in the breakfast nook, my hair coated with salad ingredients, my feet propped up on the table for a strawberry scrub. "My sugar bowl is not your personal supply of cleansing grains," she sighed. "My tea is not your steam treatment." She went on some more, but her pleas were muffled by the terry cloth tent over my head.

My family could scoff all they liked. I believed in what I was doing. My faith in a beauty regime was so absolute at these times that I thought there was nothing a good makeover couldn't cure. When I was in eighth grade my best friend and I decided that a new look was all one particularly unpopular classmate needed. We invited her over to my house for a day of spa treatments. "This is a onetime thing, Lorene," we told her. "We're not going to be best friends after this or anything. But we think we can help you."

The memory shames me now, but at the time I was quite pleased with myself for coming up with the idea. Here was a way to combine my two hobbies, beauty and good works. I'd found my cause. If this went well, I would become a door-to-door missionary for Avon and dedicate my weekends to doing pro bono work for the acne-scarred.

In spite of my insensitive invitation, Lorene graciously accepted. It went downhill from there. She had scoliosis, but we treated her as though she were uncommonly retarded.

"Here's a product called 'a-strin-gent,'" I explained slowly as we sat by the pool, the patio table covered with beauty supplies. "And here's how you use it." I mimed a swipe over my T-zone with a cotton ball. "I'm sure this seems very complicated and foreign to you right now, but you'll get the hang of it in no time."

Lorene's posture may have been impaired, but her manners, certainly, were much better than mine. Resisting the urge to remind me that she was in all my honors classes, she cheerfully replied that she'd gotten the hang of it some years ago and already used it twice a day.

I was puzzled. If she was already using a toner, why wasn't she more popular?

"Next you'll want to 'ex-fo-li-ate,' with a gentle scrub like this apricot kernel paste."

Lorene informed us that her dermatologist had told her to avoid exfoliants — she had a dermatologist? — but said she'd defer to our advanced knowledge.

Next we gave a presentation on choosing figure-flattering clothes and the importance of a healthy diet. After that, we enjoyed a break over fruit plates and iced tea. Finally we did her hair and painted her flushed, overstimulated face with a coat of makeup.

"That looks nice," she agreed when we held a mirror up to her face. "*Vogue* says that blondes like me really can't get away with burgundy eye shadow, but look at that, you proved them wrong. Thank you so much for all you taught me today. I'll be sure to incorporate your tips into my routine."

Monday arrived and nothing changed. She was wearing lip gloss, but she was tortured as usual by the slack-jawed preteen Pol Pots who shared our homeroom. How was this possible? We had exfoliated! We had toned! We had *made over!* Why was she still unpopular? I felt like a jerk and winced with embarrassment every time I saw her. In high school I was relieved when we were in few of the same classes. I avoided her in the halls, and we never spoke of the incident again.

After that spa day I wasn't the same. If anyone got a make-over, it was me. I'd become a nonbeliever. Beauty treatments lost their magic; makeup, its appeal. Now I rarely wear anything more than root beer lip gloss, and then only because I secretly like to eat it. My hair-care routine is limited to weekly brushings and biannual self-administered haircuts. Several years ago I was hired to write a series of beauty features for teenagers, and my friends were baffled. "Have your editors ever seen you?" they demanded. "Do they know you wash your hair with bar soap?"

That my campaign to change Lorene's life might fail had never occurred to me. Until then I had had complete trust in the power of cosmetics to transform and repair. Everyone does, deep down. In my twenties I liked to hang out at the CVS in Harvard Square, watching our country's premier students use their massive brainpower to spend forty-five minutes picking out a conditioner, all of them convinced that the right formula had the power to make their lives perfect and whole.

But I understood. That's what this was, the cosmetics and the compulsions, all of it an attempt to be perfect, to live a perfect life in which nobody died or had bad skin. Sometimes conditioner was the key and sometimes compulsions were. They were both variations on a theme.

Obsessive-compulsive disorders foster a strange relationship with one's body. You're constantly coming after it with tweezers and antibacterials. It is part enemy, part endless pastime. It is always giving you something to do and to dominate.

Mine kept me plenty busy. My body was unpredictable, and most of my compulsions — picking, dieting, washing — were an attempt to exert control over this thing I couldn't trust. I had no faith in it at all. It flushed and stumbled and refused to do my bidding. Where were the prominent cheekbones I had tried so hard to coax out? Where were the long tapered fingers? The shapely legs? What was this large mole doing on my forehead? Why the big yellow teeth?

I could not trust that my body would do what I wanted. I was grateful for the involuntary bodily processes that didn't require my input, but I didn't trust those, either, as I secretly believed that I could, accidentally and against my will, make my heart stop beating with my scarily potent mental powers.

Bodies break. Cosmetics could only do so much, and then it seemed they could do nothing at all. It was useless, all of it, nothing more than smoke and mirrors. Makeup could guarantee you an attractive open-casket funeral, maybe, but it couldn't bring the corpse back to life. It couldn't stop you from dying in the first place.

Why do we call bodies temples? They're a mess. My body was just a disaster. Everything was wrong, and new wrongs sprung up all the time: stray hairs, warts, broken veins, all signs, surely, that something was very screwed up, that I was sick, and worse than that, too short to model.

Once, when I was thirteen, I woke up and I couldn't smile. This is not allegory. I woke up one day and found that half of my face was paralyzed. It was the strangest thing. The right side curved up in a grin when I asked it to, but the left wouldn't move. At first my parents thought I was faking. Several lopsided grins later they were convinced, if amused. "Oh, do it again," they urged. "Hoo. That is one funny expression."

After I indulged their requests to demonstrate my frown and my surprised look, they took me to a doctor. It turned out to be nothing too serious; I had Bell's palsy was all. It's a fairly benign paralysis of the facial nerves caused, in my case, by a cold. A month or so later it went away on its own and I could smile again, if you gave me something to smile about. But it was weird and unsettling while it lasted. Roseanne Barr had the same thing when she was a child, and it inspired her Jewish family to convert temporarily to Mormonism. I could see how it could scare you into doing something like that. I could see how disease could shake your faith.

We were at war, my body and I, and all these years later we still haven't signed a truce. Perhaps it's because my body failed me so spectacularly so many times before, when the connections in my brain went haywire, when my face froze, when my bones poked out and my skin turned funny colors. The scrupulosity and anorexia eventually went away, but the profound hypochondria remained. I call my father every week with new diagnoses: I am pretty sure there are blood clots in my legs; I think my pancreas has stopped working; this mole is suspicious; these crow's feet are cancerous. It is a fact that I got my father to spend an entire Thanksgiving weekend on the phone with the Centers for Disease Control when I became convinced that I had contracted German measles and then passed it on to a pregnant friend (it was a rash). My brain works more or less as it's supposed to these days, but this part, the psychosomatic part, never got fixed.

But I am trying. I am trying very hard to trust my body, even when it twitches and throbs, when it develops new and unflattering properties like skin tags and varicose veins.

I am trying. And I believe I have a good plan. Nothing, I think, would restore my faith like some plastic work. Cosmetics weren't the answer, but I'm hopeful that cosmetic surgery might be. I've been browsing, window-shopping, testing the waters with my HMO.

It's a good idea, I think. And when I gaze upon creation through doe-like eyes, offering praise through full, shapely lips, I know my faith will be restored. It will be complete. It will be perfect.

BEAUTY TIPS FOR FASTIDIOUS GIRLS

Brows and Lashes

Nature has hardwired us to find symmetry beautiful. *Parity* and *pretty* even sound alike. They're practically the same word! So ask yourself: are your brows and lashes perfectly even? Probably not! Go ahead and count them. Count again, just to be sure. Then get out those tweezers and fix that inequality. Count again. Even yet? Okay, tweeze some more. Keep going until you're satisfied. And remember, it's better to err on the side of excess — they'll always grow back!

Scent

The well-put-together lady knows that a fresh scent is the best calling card there is. But it's not enough to smell clean — you have to *be* clean! Really, really, really clean! That's where the topical antibacterials come in. Back in the old days, the germ-conscious girl was stuck smelling like 409. But now topical antibacterials are available in a whole range of scents. Gardenia, citrus, cinnamon — it's your choice!

Hair

Sigh. What girl *doesn't* hate her hair? The flyaways, the split ends, the cowlicks, the incitement to licentiousness, the patches picked bald . . . Hair is sex and touching and death. Cover it. Just cover it.

Scars and Scabs

If you're washing fifty, a hundred times a day, cracking and bleeding are just a fact of life. But it's nothing to be ashamed of. Think of your battle wounds as Good Hygiene Medals of Honor you wear right on your skin. And a scab, a scab is just a ruby you grow yourself. The best part: it will give you something to pick at when you don't have any eyelashes left!

Skin

Feeling a little chapped but worried your whole family will die if you use a commercial moisturizer? Not to worry — there's an alternative. Just reach for a nice, hygienic, hermetically sealed bottle of salad oil. It's the moisturizer the biblical matriarchs used! Anoint yourself, for you are the chosen, it's you it's you please don't let them die. Now, doesn't that feel better?

Orange Girl

SOMETIME DURING MY junior year of high school I turned orange. I was not the first student to do so — there had been some other examples, all involving mishaps with that early generation of sunless self-tanners — but I was the first one to achieve a full-body neon effect. Everything but my eyes, teeth, and hair took on the jaundiced hue of a wilting tiger lily. In short order I had a new nickname, "Orange Girl," and an appointment with my pediatrician.

The examination was brief. "She's orange, all right," the doctor agreed. A few questions later he ascertained what was wrong. I'd been eating little besides carrots and cantaloupe. The overdose of carotene had resulted in carotenosis, a relatively harmless condition in which the skin turns a deep yellowish orange. As far as pigmentation goes, it turns out the you-are-what-you-eat axiom is pretty literal. It's a diet of shrimp that makes flamingos pink, of reddish crustaceans that makes salmon salmon. I wasn't too happy with my current predicament — I looked bad in orange — but I was excited about the possibilities. Green really brought out my eyes. I wondered what a lot of broccoli could do for me. Or plums. I looked good in plum. In the meantime, the doctor suggested I find something else to eat and sent me home.

This wasn't the outcome my family had been hoping for. After a couple years of relatively normal eating habits, I had gone off the rails again and now I was driving everyone nuts. I had adopted a typical anorexic ploy: wolf down the noncaloric foods, then, when it came time to eat the deadly lasagne, the unthinkable potatoes au gratin, plead fullness. "No macaroni for me, thanks," I demurred, patting my stomach. "After all those capers, I couldn't eat another bite!"

My meals came to consist mostly of garnish. I attacked anything wearing a frilly toothpick with a gusto that revolted my dining companions. My family learned to look away as I gnawed melon down to the rind, salted and peppered the decorative lettuce leaf, and nearly frenched the ornamental orange slices. "I don't know what you're doing to that pepperoncini, but I think you should send it some flowers tomorrow," my sister muttered. Pickles, parsley, cocktail onions — this was my diet. I could make an entire dinner out of bar fruit.

It was the carrots with ketchup and mustard that really did Vicky in. She watched with distaste as I ate them every afternoon.

"They're nature's french fries," I told her.

"My ass they are," she returned. "For once can't you fix yourself a snack that doesn't look like it's been fished out of the compost pile? Try aiming a little higher up the food chain, retard. People aren't supposed to eat this way." She must have been delighted when my complexion conspired to prove her right.

Not that it did her much good. My family had expected I would leave the doctor's office with a stern rebuke and, if things went really well, a prescription for tranquilizers that I might agree to share with my more pharmaceutically adventurous kin. My mother frowned when I bounded out into the waiting room without so much as a pamphlet.

"Did he weigh you?" she demanded, folding her arms across her chest and tapping her foot aggressively. "Did you tell him what you've been eating? Did you tell him you haven't had a period in a year and a half and I don't have a grandchild to show for it?"

"Yes, yes, and yes," I lied, snapping a piece of sugarless gum. "He says I'm normal."

My mother rolled her eyes. "Yeah, well, I'm onto you. You may have fooled him, but I know you're not right."

She had a point. I was orange. Of course something was wrong. I was marked with highlighter, like an important passage in an abnormal-psych textbook, like a glaring accusation of bad parenting. I was a neon beacon of teen dysfunction. On the plus side, it was unlikely I'd accidentally get shot by a hunter.

The other plus was that I was a shoo-in for school mascot. Our school colors were orange and white. At football games our bleachers looked like a front porch on November first, a sea of smashed pumpkin. I never learned who was to blame for this lapse of taste. Perhaps a previous class had been allowed to vote on it. How they must have laughed when they sentenced us to wear colors that would make us look like pimply Muppets for all eternity.

Or perhaps a cruel principal was responsible. Only a sadistic mad-man could have chosen hues guaranteed to flatter exactly no one's complexion. At our school, every day was Salloween.

It was a color combination that aroused nausea and dread but not spirit. Well, nausea and dread have their uses. This was some-thing of which the school's planners had been well aware. De-signed by a Foucauldian architect to discourage vandalism, the campus resembled nothing so much as a prison. It did not have a single window or skylight. It was less a campus than a compound, with high sandstone walls and retractable iron gates that stood at the ready should a total lockdown ever be required. In my junior year a classmate flipped out and killed three people in the country-side. At the sentencing the district attorney warned him that he didn't know what he was in for: "Prison is nothing like Woodland High." Was he nuts? Prison was *exactly* like Woodland High. The inmates even wore the same color. Fifteen years later, when the town finally got big enough to require a second high school, they went ahead and built it right next to the jail.

In 1973 the campus had been considered the height of mod-ern architecture and served as the setting for a TV movie about high school football called *Blood Sport*. It starred Gary Busey and Larry Hagman and, to my everlasting delight, my algebra teacher. The film was about a quarterback who was torn between his father and his coach, and the prisonlike structure of the school underscored the movie's rock-and-a-hard-place message. Curi-ously, the only other movie filmed in my hometown also had a prison setting. It was called *The Stunt Man* and featured Peter O'Toole and Barbara Hershey. We went down to watch the film-ing at the old jailhouse. I believe Mr. O'Toole was already on the wagon at that point, but we were inclined to believe the worst when we saw him weaving out of his trailer while Barbara held him up. "She's Jewish," my mother stage-whispered to me. "That's probably why she's sober."

I knew how she felt. I, too, was soberly shouldering a staggering burden, but instead of an Oscar-nominated actor it was nameless dread. It was just normal teenage angst — oh, and some fairly serious brain dysfunction — but I wore it badly. I was convinced that I'd stumbled into the wrong life, and maybe I had. I was a neurotic Jewish kid. I was supposed to be off at some forward-thinking East Coast boarding school experimenting with lesbianism and casual drug use. Instead I was at Hillbilly High, an agricultural voc-ed school meant to prepare kids to take over their parents' farms.

And for this, it was very good. The school was not without its merits and strong suits. But the closest thing my parents had to a farm was a browning front lawn. I didn't belong there. This was a school that didn't teach Latin, Creative Writing, or AP anything, but did offer Advanced Gunsmithing and Animal Husbandry. In May it was not uncommon to see a girl in taffeta and heels using the gun rack to hoist herself into her prom date's monster truck. Future Farmers of America was by far the largest club on campus, and hay-baling competitions and pig-kissing contests were normal school events. One morning between classes I found my best friend clutching her abdomen and trying to suppress a gag reflex. "The Ag kids were castrating sheep in homeroom," she explained, her eyes watering. "I know you won't believe me, but I swear they did it with their teeth."

No wonder I was unhappy. There was college to look forward to, but if my teachers were any indication, adulthood was no party. Oh, sure, most of my instructors were serious, well-adjusted educators who presented their subjects with enthusiasm, who took us out for sodas after school, and who really cared about their students' welfare. But there was also a fair share of alcoholics, fading beauties, and other bitter malcontents. Our female teachers tended to begin class with the warning "I've got cramps like you wouldn't believe, so if you kids are smart you won't mess with me today."

Looking back on it now, I can't believe I didn't have more fun. Sheep and prison bars — this was rich stuff. But I lacked the exotic sexual proclivities or sense of humor that would have made my high school experience a good time. All I had was a bad attitude and an eating disorder.

That, and a very full schedule. I was extremely busy trying to get into a good college. Warned that good grades from my high school wouldn't mean much, I was desperate to pad my résumé with activities. I joined every club I could. French Club? Oui! Student Council? Aye! Literary Club, Service Club, Honor Society, Scholarship Foundation — I joined any group that didn't require interaction with livestock or my sister. I went to Mecha meetings until I was gently reminded that the club was actually for Chicano students. Well, fine, I'd stop coming, but would they mind if I put it on my CV anyway? Multicultural candidates really had an edge.

I have never been an easy person, but I can say with confidence that at no point in my life was I as all-around unpleasant as I was my junior year. With the exception of a few close and patient friends, the only people who would put up with me were the ones trying to pad their own college applications. We didn't want someone to hang out with — we wanted someone to delegate to. Constantly dispensing World's Finest fund-raising chocolate bars, we were a league of human vending machines, cold and efficient. My sister could barely contain her scorn reading the chilly inscriptions they wrote in my yearbook. "Listen to this one," she snorted. "It's like a letter of recommendation. 'Jenny: You have many wonderful talents and I hope you'll make the most of them. You are thorough and responsible. Thanks for always being there when I needed a'" — Vicky paused, convulsed with laughter — "'a Secretary/Treasurer.'"

In what anyone could have interpreted as a cry for help, I even joined the Drama Club. I can't imagine what possessed me to join these ranks. I didn't sing, dance, or act, and I couldn't have thought it was actually going to help me get into college. Maybe I was working out some hostility toward my family by forcing them to come to show after agonizing show, including one production of *South Pacific* that was so bad even the cast referred to it as "South Pathetic."

I stank up the stage pretty good all on my own. Mousy and shy, I was always cast against type as an adenoidal moll. My family visibly winced listening to me practice my lines. "Shuuwah, honey," I brayed. "I can get yuh the infahmation. But it'll cost yuh!" My costumes were invariably skimpy and tight, a real liability when we had to wear them to school to promote the show. The worst was from the "Bushel and a Peck" number in *Guys and Dolls*. I had to spend an entire school day in a halter top, obscenely tight cutoffs with a heart patch on the rear, fishnet stockings, and black high heels. My mother eyed me warily as I tottered off to class. "You know, I saw the film version, and I don't remember the role of 'Barnyard Slut,'" she said, rolling her irises all the way back.

Four-inch heels aside, I was clearly unstable, and my stint in the Drama Club prompted my parents to look into getting me some help. Washing and praying were fine, but acting and singing — that was too much. They made some calls. I eavesdropped nervously. Was this the incident that would finally land me in therapy? Should I start working on a tearful first-visit monologue?

In the end, my parents made an appointment with a dietician instead. That was even better: it meant I was troubled *and* thin. Secretly I was pleased; secretly I'd been disappointed when my orange skin had failed to result in a hospital stay. I was being taken seriously. Now there were specialists. Now it was official.

I saw the dietician two or three times and enjoyed the visits enormously. Her office had fun-house mirrors that let you see yourself fat and thin. There were plastic foods to show reasonable portion sizes and latex models of orange, glistening fat. It was all very interesting, and best of all, I got to spend an hour talking about the most fascinating thing in the world, my eating habits.

They were very bad, it turned out. The dietitian did her best to put a scare in me. I was jeopardizing my health. I would develop anemia, osteoporosis, and possibly organ failure. I was already orange, and things were only going to get worse. I had to stop this nonsense.

I ate up the attention, but I had no intention of changing my habits or of admitting there was a problem. I wasn't trying to lose weight, I offered coyly. I just didn't have time to eat, what with all my rehearsals, you know, life on the wicked stage. The dietitian gave me a withering look that suggested I wasn't as good an actress as I thought I was and resignedly sent me on my way.

Shortly thereafter my mother decided to take her own show on the road. It was just a brief trip back East to help move her elderly aunts, but it couldn't have come at a better time. With my mother gone, I could take my eating disorder in the exciting new direction I'd been contemplating for a while. Well, it wasn't so new. It was the exact same thing I'd done four years earlier. Once again, I was becoming increasingly bothered by the idea of contamination. There was so much unkosher food in the house. How could I be sure it wasn't creeping into my meals? I could not, and I was going to have to do something about it. This was crazy, of course, but in my defense I would like to point out that my sister had a lifelong history of tainting others' food, a hobby her future career as a waitress would give her plenty of opportunities to indulge. Though it's strictly an after-hours, avocational hobby now, she has, in the distant past, served up plenty of sneezers. She once dealt with a difficult vegan patron by surreptitiously stirring his beer with bacon. In high school she worked at a pizza parlor, where she hid pepperoni in the pies ordered by a snotty vegetarian classmate. I have seen her serve her own friends salsa seasoned with cigarette ash and cookies she licked simply because she was bored. Sometimes she just can't help herself.

With a sister who couldn't be trusted and parents who were finally, if temporarily, busy elsewhere, I decided to limit my diet to hermetically sealed processed-cheese singles and a low-calorie bread whose chief ingredient was wood pulp. Of course, neither one of these items was actually kosher or, for that matter, actually food, but for some reason they satisfied my concerns.

My sister, meanwhile, was marking my mother's absence the way normal teenagers do, toasting it with a few wine coolers. The night before my mother was due to come home, my father got a 2:00 a.m. call asking him to come down to the police station to pick up his drunk, sticky daughter. Apparently a cop had found Vicky and a friend lying on a curb outside a party, and he'd been unimpressed when they introduced themselves as Vicky Bartles and Lori Jaymes.

Vicky and I had visited no end of humiliations on our parents, but "juvy" was a new one. Our parents had forbidden a host of things they were sure would lead right to delinquency — pierced ears, camping, beef jerky — and now their efforts had come to naught. Their daughter had a rap sheet. In the end, Vicky's minor infraction would be erased after a court appearance and a couple visits with a juvenile officer, but at the time we were fairly convinced she was one kegger away from an orange jumpsuit herself. We pictured ourselves visiting her in the Big House. "We would have brought you a carton of cigarettes, but we think it's better you learn to fend for yourself," we would say. "If you want a smoke, you'll have to earn it giving lap dances to the guards like the other girls do."

My father informed my mother of my sister's misadventure on the way home from the airport. My mother nodded, came in the house, and put on the bathrobe she would wear for the next week, refusing to speak to anyone but Saint Jude. Between the drinking and the sleepwear, it was as if my family had been replaced by a road company of *Cat on a Hot Tin Roof.*

Well, at least it took the heat off me. I had a lot going on and was pleased that I would be left unmolested. Goodness knows I had enough to do. Besides all my extracurricular activities, I had returned to some old hobbies: fervent praying, repetitive washing, and writing theological manifestos. I couldn't help myself. I began to pray more and more, spending a minimum of two hours a day perched under a yarmulke on a makeshift pew, rocking and whispering the half-cocked devotions I'd composed myself. "Please help me to be a better person. Please save the Ethiopians from starving. Please forgive me for wearing Daisy Dukes to school," I implored. If I felt I hadn't said my prayers in the right order or with the proper thoughts in mind, I would have to repeat them. When I finished with that, I filled my diary with strange, keening entries: "How amazing is it that the Jewish people have survived? Jenny, when you are feeling down, remember this!!!!!!!!"

I was up writing, cleaning, and praying until midnight, then rose at dawn to begin the three hours of writing, cleaning, and praying I had to do before school. In my free time, I rewashed clean dishes. It was a full and exciting life.

By Passover, it was clear that the problems I'd had earlier were back in a big way. I was hip-deep in a full-blown flare-up, and this time it was much worse. My previous experiences with scrupulosity had been mostly compulsive — I washed, I performed odd rituals — but not particularly obsessive. Except for my annual summer flare-up, I hadn't been plagued by ruminations, the disturbing thoughts that can consume OCD sufferers. This time, however, ruminations hijacked my life.

What would happen was this: I would be struck by a pressing theological question, like "Is it okay to sit at my assigned desk when there's a strong possibility it was contaminated by the skank who occupies it during second period?" I would have to re-solve the question before I did anything else, like move or speak. It was a neurotic's version of freeze tag. If I messed up and, say, scratched my nose before I'd resolved my theological quandary, I would have to think the whole question through again, until I resolved it without interruption. At that point I would invariably be struck by another pressing question: "Is it okay to watch this educational film strip or is *The Miracle of Digestion* in fact a graven image?"

Before long I developed the stuttering walk that's so typical of OCD sufferers. Some can't walk contiguously because they're afraid of stepping on cracks or crosses or blood. I couldn't walk because I would become paralyzed by a theological question that had to be resolved before I put left foot in front of right. It could take me half an hour to cross the quad. Conversation became impossible. I would break off in the middle of sentences, knit my brow, and set my mind to the question at hand: "Is cologne kosher, and if it's not, is it okay to talk to someone who's wearing so much Love's Baby Soft I can taste it?"

Unable to focus in class, I would wander out, only to be found rocking and muttering in the outdoor amphitheater. Being in Drama Club was finally coming in handy. When questioned, I could simply explain that I was "getting in character." "You see, Mr. Davis, I'm playing a hooker who's trying to 'kick.' I was just out here trying to imagine what it must be like to have the DTs." Then I would begin contemplating the next quandary: "Does the Torah say it's okay to portray a hooker, and is a heart of gold a mitigating factor?"

This behavior wasn't going to help me get into a good college, I realized, but I couldn't help it. Besides, what did college matter when we were all going to die, when everything was contaminated and dirty with death? This had suddenly become a real preoccupation, the taint of corpses. The Torah has a lot to say about it. A dead body is impure, imparting a contamination that's contagious, that infects not just the person who touches it, but all that that person then touches. It's a mess, and getting yourself purified is a complicated procedure that takes lots of time, high priests, livestock, and herbs.

This turns out to be another one of those things that was really only an issue in Temple times, but I didn't know that. And in my case the impurity was a legitimate concern. Most teenage girls don't have all that many run-ins with dead bodies, but I was the daughter of a surgeon. My father was contaminated all the time, and he brought contamination home with him. It infected the chairs and the doorknobs, the dishes and the floors. It was everywhere.

Even independent of my father, I had run-ins of my own. I was taking Anatomy, and sometimes there were body parts. They were usually animal, which was bad enough, but sometimes they were human, which was unthinkable. One day a friend placed a human skull on my binder. It was just a harmless joke, but as far as I was concerned she might as well have taken a giant dump on it or sprinkled it with anthrax. This was the worst possible contamination and there was no help for it. I could not throw the binder away, as it contained all the notes I would need to pass the stupid class, but I couldn't let the impurity stand. I agonized for days. In the end I wiped the binder down with bleach and 409 a few hundred times, then placed it on the guest bed in my room. The bed, in turn, absorbed the impurity, and in my mind it hung on to it long after I'd passed my final and thrown the binder away. The taboo against touching that bed remained so deeply entrenched that it was as though someone had died on the bed itself, and almost twenty years later I still can't bring myself to sleep in it.

Everywhere I looked, there was dirt and death, contamination and sin and wrongness. By May I was vibrating, a quivering mass of misfiring neurons. I couldn't sit still; I couldn't walk; I couldn't sustain a single activity for more than a few seconds. I couldn't do my homework or pay attention in class. And I was starting to look very, very weird. My skin had returned to its normal freakishly pale tone, but everything else had gone wonky. I'd given up all grooming products on the assumption that they were unkosher. "Unless you plan to eat the stick of deodorant, it's probably okay to use it," my father argued, but I was unconvinced. OCD is hell on the complexion, what with all the washing, and without the benefit of balms and emollients my lips split and bled, my hands cracked and wept, my hair frizzed. A Jewish girl just can't go without conditioner; "Thou shalt use a heat pack weekly" is the unspoken eleventh commandment. Without styling tools my already pneumatic mall hair quickly degenerated into a shaggy, damaged Jewfro, carrying enough static electricity to power a waffle iron.

When I lost my glasses, a stylish and expensive pair I'd picked out before I went daft, I felt obliged to punish myself by replacing them with the most age-inappropriate pair I could find. They were enormous, covering a full half of my face, with peach Lucite frames. I believe they were from the Sophia Loren collection; only Sophia could have pulled them off. With my hair, I ended up looking like Gene Shalit.

To make matters worse, I'd decided most of my wardrobe was impure. If it had been washed on Shabbat, it was out. If it had touched something that had been washed on Shabbat, it was out. If it had been touched by an insect, worn to a place where someone or something had died, including an insect, or worn during the commission of what I would now consider a sin, it was out. It was also out if it was made from more than one fiber. The Torah bans garments made from a mix of linen and wool, and I extrapolated this to include any fiber combination. Call it crazy, but I still think it's a good idea to ban poly blends.

In the end I was left with a uniform consisting of some military-style pants that had fit when I was twenty pounds heavier and an enormous man's plaid flannel shirt. It was a strange choice on all counts. Religiously, it didn't make sense; Orthodox girls don't wear men's clothes. And stylewise, it was a disaster. Ten years later it might have been considered grunge, but at the time I just looked like a nearsighted Jewish chola. I so closely resembled the Mexican gang members at our high school that my friends dubbed me "La Sad Girl."

But even gang members had the sense to strip down to undershirts in the heat. I remained swathed in head-to-toe flannel. One sweltering afternoon my mother and I sat watching a talk show whose topic was "My Teen Dresses Too Sexy." "Take notes, Jenny," my mother suggested. "Don't those girls look nice and cool? I like the one in the red vinyl number with the cut-outs over the chest and fanny. You'd look good in something like that."

It was around this time that I became a real social liability. Sure, my parents could try to bring me to the neighbors' house for a dinner party, but there was a pretty good chance that halfway through the meal they would find me in the front yard, using the garden hose to wash an invisible contaminant off my feet. You never knew what I was going to do, and you could be sure I was going to wear something that would require extensive explanations. "It's quite a look, isn't it, this military getup?" my mother would offer. "It's Jenny's costume for the school play. She's playing a Vietnamese commando, and they've got her in character 'round the clock. It's a 'method' thing. Now, come on, My Le, let's get you out of the Taylors' flower bed and into some dry socks."

After a month or so of this, my parents decided the school year was over for me. School was almost out, anyway, and there was no point in taking finals. Unless I was asked to answer an essay question about, say, the Torah's position on fungal infections, there was no way I was going to pass. My teachers were very nice about the whole thing. Frankly, I think they were relieved to have me out of the classroom. Between the hooker costumes, the fund-raising chocolate, and the muttering, I'd been a distraction all year.

It was early June and my summer had begun. I wasn't happy about the incompletes, but the unstructured time, the endless hours to spend as I liked, that was wonderful. I woke up the first morning and smiled at the reflection of Gene Shalit in the mirror. I was free. I could do whatever I wanted. It was a beautiful day and I was going to get right out there and enjoy it, just as soon as I finished inspecting this toothbrush.

SAMPLE SAT QUESTIONS
FOR OBSESSIVE-COMPULSIVE LEARNERS

1. SUN : BURN ::
   A. DOORKNOB : DISEASE
   B. LIGHT SWITCH : FIRE
   C. EVEN NUMBERS : DEATH
   D. You see? There's a pattern. I'm not making this up. You see? You see?

2. The cheese's pungent _____ permeated the kitchen.
   A. Effluvia
   B. Sometimes I wrap things in plastic and hide them.
   C. Pusillanimity
   D. Feculence

3. Solve for x.
   $x(3x) + 2(2(4 - x)) = 20$
   A. $x = 1$
   B. $x = 2$
   C. x = a cross. Answering this question is tantamount to converting to Christianity. Leave blank. Don't even circle the C. Just move on to the next question.
   D. $x = 4$

4. James has three sisters and two oranges. One sister is twice as hungry as the other two, and each orange has sixteen sections. How many times must James tap the fruit to make sure his sisters don't die? Show your work.

A. 3 (once for each sister)

B. 9 (three times for each sister)

C. 18 (three times for each sister, times two for each orange)

D. 90 (three times for each sister, times two for each orange, repeated until taps are performed with perfect concentration, a feat finally achieved on the fifth attempt)

Sacre Bleu

LIKE MANY GIRLS who don't get asked out in high school, I spent my teenage years believing I was a displaced European. It was so obvious I'd been born in the wrong country, what with my having such sophisticated Continental sensibilities and all. As soon as I was old enough, I told myself and anyone who would listen, I was moving to a country where my unconventional looks, difficult charms, and erratic hygiene would be appreciated.

That country was France. I always felt I'd been cheated of the French citizenship that was rightfully mine, a birthright sold for a mess of *potage*. My father's parents had met and married in France, had gone to school and given birth to their first child there, had planned to make it their home forever, and then had the good sense to get out. France has always had its anti-Semitic elements, and by the late 1930s it was about as Jew friendly as a

Klan pig roast. They moved to a French colony in Shanghai. Even French Jews, it turns out, have a thing for Chinese food.

There, they saddled their children with French names and educations in anticipation of a speedy return. The plan was to go back to Paris as soon as the war was over and Hermès was open again. My grandparents were lawyers, and while their French citizenship qualified them to judge all the world's citizens, their French law degrees permitted them to practice law only in France. Where else could they live?

California, it turns out. A brief stopover on the way back to Paris turned into a permanent stay. The decision was made as soon as they changed the family name from Treguboff to the Americanized Traig, which, when said with a French accent, is exactly the sound one makes when clearing one's sinuses. Their children adopted American nicknames, lost their accents, and stopped ironing their jeans. By the time I was born, the only French affectations the family retained were a postprandial salad course and a fondness for scarves.

Instead of being raised on goat cheese, I was raised on a goat farm. Instead of Gaul, gall. Oh, it just wasn't fair. Still, I tried. I might not have the French citizenship but, *sacre bleu*, I would have the superciliousness. I adopted a superior attitude as soon as I was old enough to look down my nose at the other toddlers. I was a shamelessly affected child, given to uttering phrases like "Oh, Papa, do please read me *The Little Prince — en français.*" He indulged me, but my mother only sighed and shook her head when I asked her to replace the Pop-Tart in my lunch with a fruit and cheese course. "You keep this up, mademoiselle, and I'm pulling you out of ballet and signing you up for Four-H."

I kept it up. I wore berets. I played soccer. By age nine, I was trying to teach myself French from a 1950s Berlitz, useful for phrases like "This sedan rides as smoothly as a couch," but not much else. Even my grandfather — a man who wore ascots — thought I was taking it too far. "You are learning Fransh?" he demanded in the melodic Continental accent I so envied. "But thees ees ridiculeux! Look at thees *village* you leeve in! They barely speak English, never mind *Fransh*. A course in *l'agronomie* will be so much more useful to you here."

He was probably right. By the time I was in high school it was clear that the only people who would listen to me were the exchange students, and, like everything else in my life thus far, they disappointed me. I had been hoping for a dashing Jewish Rothschild to swoop into my homeroom and propose to me on the spot. "Never in my life have I met a girl so fastidious, so pure, so *charmante*," he would declare, taking my chapped hand in his. "Now, come with me, my little Hebrew flower. I'm taking you back to the garden where you belong."

Mais non. Instead of Alain Delon and Catherine Deneuve we got a cavalcade of misfits as pimply and badly dressed as we were. Europe was clearly exporting its least attractive adolescents to my high school. I began to suspect they were not being exchanged but exiled, for not being pretty enough to live in their native countries. They were being sent to America to mate with more appropriate partners, like the poor souls with cystic acne and self-inflicted haircuts who made up much of our student body.

Still, there were a few lookers who managed to slip through. We swooned over Guy, the fey French flight attendant who'd somehow landed in our town. Bored and lonely, with nothing better to do than hang out with high school kids, Guy sometimes modeled in our teen fashion shows, captivating us all with his husky accent and Gallic cheekbones. The boys fell for Solange, the nubile *jeune fille* who spent summers with some family friends. Solange spoke not a word of English and had to be forcibly restrained from walking down the street topless. At fourteen, she was already on the pill. We gaped, chuckled, shook our heads: Oh, those French. They are such sluts. What can you do?

Even in my scrupulous periods, I remained a devoted Francophile. Oh, sure, I knew the French were a bunch of libidinous heathens. My cousin had shared his French dorm-mate's description of a date: "She was a *peeg*. She bite my *derrière*. But what could she do? I was seeting on her face!" I knew. But they were so charming I couldn't hold it against them. I might have felt differently if I'd ever actually been there. The closest I'd come to France was Canada, which is France with better manners and worse clothes, France as performed in Branson, Missouri. It doesn't count.

The summer I turned seventeen I would finally get to see the real thing. My family was going to Paris. What was making this possible was the bottle of pills in my father's breast pocket. They were tiny, no bigger than a teen bride's diamond, but they could keep me quiet for six hours at a stretch. This was our passport. This would keep me docile and compliant in the face of bloody *saucissons* and medieval bathrooms, oyster bars and leering, unwashed men, and, worse than all these, the horrors continually invented in my own brain.

In college I would pay good money for any pill that could do that, but at the time I wasn't having it, not at all. After years of full-blown crazy-making and an extraordinary end-of-junior-year meltdown I was finally in therapy, lots of it, and though I liked talking about myself for hours on end, I was not happy about the pharmaceutical component.

"Drugs," my parents had insisted at my intake session. "Let's get her on drugs. Freudian, Jungian, we don't care what you are as long as you believe in Percodan, Ativan, or Vicodin. Just give her some meds."

I was vehemently against this plan. OCD and anorexia revolve around controlling the body and what goes into it, and this control was not something I was eager to relinquish. Frizzy hair and orange skin aside, my body was the one thing I had achieved a measure of control over. But one little pill could have me flinging off my underwear to join Solange sunbathing on the lawn, waving at the cars that slowed as they passed. No, thanks.

I was appalled. Nancy Reagan was still in the White House, and her big red *No* was tattooed on my brain. No, no, of course no. Though I went to school with lots of drug dealers' kids, who crowded their friends into the bathroom stalls between classes, snorting and cackling, I'd never actually been offered a mind-altering substance before. I had been preparing for this moment all my life. I had rehearsed the lines I would say, from the self-righteous, "Drugs aren't cool!" to the stealth denial, "No, thanks, man, I'm already too baked." I just couldn't believe I was going to have to say them to my parents.

We battled over the issue for several weeks. In the end we agreed I would not take medication every day, but only when I was "acting up" — a condition to be determined by my father — at which point I was taking the pill even if they had to administer it rectally.

Considering the colonic treatments that used to be prescribed for OCD, I got off easy with the pills. The mid-eighties were still the dark ages as far as OCD was concerned. Though I had a textbook case, I was not told what I had or what caused it. I'm not sure my therapist even knew. Like many sufferers, I hid it, even from my shrink; it was just too embarrassing. Better she should think I was bipolar or borderline or, as one doctor suggested I might be, schizophrenic. Auditory hallucinations — there's no shame there. But washing your hands a hundred times a day is just *crazy*.

Even if my therapist did know what I had, it was unlikely I'd get very effective treatment. All the wonderful drugs we have now weren't available then. The prevailing treatment was behavior modification, and let's face it, that's just too much work.

But there were some pills. Now it's treated with selective serotonin reuptake inhibitors like Prozac, but then we got tranquilizers. These were not particularly effective. They don't knock out the compulsion; they knock out the compulsive. But that's something. Had they been given to the compulsive's family as well, you'd have had a pretty good working solution.

So we had the drugs and we were going to France. Or so we hoped; this was a season of half-starts. My erratic behavior had been forcing my family to cancel plans fairly consistently. Dinners out, weekends away — we'd be ready to go and then something would happen; I would step in something contaminated or touch something unsafe and I'd lose it, sending everyone stomping back into the house. We were only two weeks into summer and I'd already bailed on Rotary Camp, three babysitting gigs, and a day trip to the state fair. If the thought of kids and corn dogs sent me into rocking catatonia, what would snails and topless beaches do?

Well, nonrefundable tickets have a way of keeping you in line. And while I seriously doubted I could handle it, I really wanted to go. Then, two weeks before we were supposed to leave, something was wrong.

What was wrong was that my abdomen had grown knives. An alien trying to claw its way out of my liver, or perhaps a wrestling match in my intestine — there was something inside me, and it was armed. All the bad things I'd ever thought I deserved were happening, right now, in my stomach. I couldn't stand up. I couldn't keep anything down. I'd been transformed into a natural wonder, a marvel, a spouting geyser of vomit and petulance.

Oh, something was wrong. It took about ten hours to convince anyone of this fact. I was the girl who cried "Wolf!" or not "Wolf!" but "Contamination!" and "Iniquity!" and "Disease!" Between my scrupulosity and my hypochondria, my family had learned to ignore my dire premonitions years earlier. Besides, some moaning and vomit were all part of a normal day's work. It would have taken bleeding ears or perhaps stigmata to elicit more than a shrug.

"Go lie down," my parents suggested. Ten hours later, when I wasn't feeling any better and my eyes had rolled all the way back in their sockets, they thought it might be a good idea to get this checked out. Yes, I thought, let's get this checked out. Too preoccupied by pain to subject my outfit to the usual inspection, I quickly slipped into a T-shirt, a skirt that fell to my hipbones, and a pair of plastic shoes, noting with some satisfaction that they all matched. I gingerly picked my way toward the car, then collapsed on the backseat and took up a moan that would not cease for the entire forty-five seconds it took us to drive the block and a half to the hospital.

When we got there we learned my father was the only surgeon on call. The same stupid hospital policy that had prevented him from giving me the cheekbone implants I'd wanted for my tenth birthday prevented him from treating me now. I would get nothing for the pain until they could locate a doctor I wasn't related to. In the meantime, perhaps I would enjoy reading this eight-year-old issue of *Field & Stream*.

I moaned and rolled my head in response. I did not want sporting magazines. I didn't even want *People*. I just wanted the meds. After spending two weeks insisting I go on drugs, now that I really, really needed them, my father was denying me. I couldn't believe it. "I think this qualifies as 'acting up!'" I shrieked.

"If I give you something now, the doctor won't be able to evaluate you properly, honey," my father answered gently. "Believe me, I would like nothing more than to take the edge off for you. For all of us. In fact, I'm sure your mother is wishing we'd had a little wine with dinner right about now. But we didn't, and you can't, and you're just going to have to take the pain."

I nodded tearfully, sat up on the examination table, placed a paper towel on my head, and prayed for the next two hours.

It was appendicitis. Of course it was appendicitis. I had it coming. The day before, I'd committed so many sins I knew something really bad was going to happen. There was going to be retribution, and I was lucky it was appendicitis and not the brain tumor I actually deserved.

I had spent the day with my best friend's family. They'd invited me sailing, and my parents had leapt at the chance to get me out of the house for a day. "It'll be great," my mother promised. "The fresh air will do you a world of good. Maybe you can start working on a tan. I bet a little sunshine is all you need to get your complexion back to a more normal tone. And if you get, you know, contaminated, you can just dip your hands over the side of the boat. Won't that be fun?"

"I don't think I can handle this," I answered.

"Uh-huh. They're picking you up at ten."

And so we set off along the Delta, a body of water known for its murky appearance and delicious seafood. As far as I was concerned, we were stewing in a giant bowl of clam chowder. This was bad enough, but trying to act normal for eight whole hours — eight hours that included two meals — that was just impossible. What was I going to eat? When was I supposed to pray? And the bugs — what about all the bugs?

I was fine for five whole minutes. Then someone offered me a soda. Oh, man, a soda. What was I supposed to do about this soda? There was probably ham in the cooler. The ham molecules had probably permeated the soda can somehow. There was no way this soda was kosher. But if I declined the soda, I might offend my hosts, and that would be a sin, too. Maybe the soda *was* kosher. Or maybe it *wasn't* a sin to decline beverages. Yes. No. Maybe. Wait. *What does the Torah say about ham-tainted carbonated beverages? What? What?*

I interrupted this line of thought to answer, "None for me, thanks," and this was the worst sin of all, interrupting a theological inquiry to talk, and I had to think about that for a while, and then I got interrupted again, and so it went all day until they dropped me off at my house, sunburned and sick with myself for being such an awful, sinful person.

So appendicitis was a light sentence. It was almost a reward, it was such a light sentence. For the next several months, I took great satisfaction in picturing the organ, red and glistening and angry, quivering and erect with toxins. I would imagine the excision and the disposal, and then I would wonder where it went and what it had taken with it. I was not sorry to have it gone.

Appendicitis wasn't bad. And if it hadn't been appendicitis it would have been something else. I was a wreck. When my sister called my friends to tell them where I was, the only surprise was that I wasn't on the psych ward. Of course I was in the hospital. Where else would I be?

Rotary Camp, that's where. And I was having much more fun in the hospital. I had worn out my parents' patience months earlier, but now I had a whole new staff to fuss over me. I couldn't wash as much as I liked, having fainted during my one attempt to shower, but I was sedated enough not to care. The food part was easy. All my parents' friends worked in the hospital. There was always someone who had missed their last meal break and was happy to help me get rid of my turkey and Jell-O salad. But they couldn't have the pudding; the pudding, I decided, was kosher. I had pudding and a remote control and push-button morphine. Paris schmaris — I wasn't going anywhere.

My HMO felt otherwise, however, and soon I was home, with a head full of ruminations and a week's worth of compulsive rituals to perform. Five days later I could walk a block, with help. Five days after that I was at the airport, leaning on my suitcase for support. We were going to France, we were going and we had the drugs. Me and my family and this bottle of pills, we were going.

The first pill was forced on me before we even lifted off. Anyone could have seen this coming. I'd spent the previous three months curled up under the coffee table crying uncontrollably. I had an angry red scar on my belly and an anesthesia hangover and I'd been ambulatory for less than a week. Oh, and I was crazy, and Orthodox, and my parents had scheduled our transatlantic flight for a Friday night.

I flipped out as soon as the preflight beverage service began. There were beverages and snacks, and it was too much. I burst out crying, knocking over my cup and sending my honey-roasted peanuts flying, a shower of legume confetti all over seats 8A through D. "Oh, yes, I think it's time for one of these," my father announced, pulling the vial out of his pocket. I argued briefly, then gave up and washed the tablet down with the remains of my diet 7-Up.

Half an hour later it kicked in, a dreamy half-buzz I would both resist and crave. It did nothing for my impulses. It did, however, distract me. It detached my head from my body, myself from my surroundings. Now it was like I was watching a movie: Oh, these beautiful people, they are so pretty, with this lovely twilight filling the cabin, so lovely, really, look how pretty my sister is, look. I watched it all unfold and it was lovely, my fellow travelers all enjoying themselves, all of us having such a good time. Look at the French couple slipping into the bathroom together, oh, those French, what can you do. I waved at them sleepily as they locked the door behind themselves, and the next thing I knew it was morning and we were on the tarmac.

Because my father is allergic to cabs, he had worked out a way to get from the airport to our accommodations using only public transportation. This was a simple procedure that required no less than two trains, a bus, and three different Metro lines, all easily navigable with sixty pounds of luggage. Two and a half hours later we staggered out into the Paris sunshine and began the ten-block march to our quarters. All along the way beautiful young French people enjoying *parfaits* and *coupes de glace* at quaint outdoor cafés gaped at the ridiculous, rumpled American family who appeared to be taking all their belongings for a walk. This was not how I had pictured my arrival — I'd been hoping for a litter, or at the very least a horse-drawn carriage, at the *very* least a *taxi* — but we were here.

We had rented an apartment in the Latin Quarter. It sounded so bohemian, so chic. "This is so much better than staying in a hotel," we told ourselves. "We'll get the real French experience." I suppose we did. The walls were paper-thin, and our fellow tenants were crazy sex fiends. Below us was a middle-aged painter whose sole hobbies were seducing shirtless ephebes thirty years his junior and attempting to kill the neighbors' cats. He was partial to poison bombs that bothered the cats not at all but forced the rest of us to evacuate with our throats closing and eyes swelling shut. Next door we had a young lady who seemed perfectly nice until the first night her boyfriend came over. Their gymnastics were conducted at full volume right next to my head. After a few days of this I was ready to dose the building's water supply with saltpeter. What was *with* these people?

It was an educational trip. Besides learning the French for "Give it to me good, you smelly bastard," I picked up quite a bit about history and physiology. The rest of my family consists of two medical professionals and a sadist, all of whom are fascinated by the gallstones, flayed scalps, and pickled genitalia of history. My idea of sightseeing is Benetton; theirs is seventeenth-century tumors. Paris is a city that indulges a morbid fascination like no other. There are museums of embryology, of torture implements, of dentistry and surgical oddities. There are bones and bugs and guillotines. My family was delighted. Each morning they would announce our itinerary over coffee and croissants. "We thought we'd start with the Catacombs, then check out the Colostomy Museum. If we have time we'll hit the Museum of Taxidermied Novelties in the afternoon." For a girl whose fear of contamination by death was such that a dead spider in my sock drawer would prompt six showers, minimum, this was quite a bit more than I could take.

My scrupulosity made even regular museums agony. I had decided not to look at any paintings of people; they were graven images, and if I was going to do that I might as well go ahead and build a golden calf. Worse still were the religious paintings, idols all. My parents had seen this coming and had warned me not to try anything funny. "If we pay eight dollars to get you into a museum you're damn well going to look at everything they have there," they insisted. I placated them by pretending to look at the artwork; I was actually just looking at the frames.

This was a great way to make a boring outing a lot less interesting. The scrupulosity was only part of the reason I didn't want to be there. The main reason was that the museums were so horribly dull. Despite my affectations, I have no interest in actual culture. I would much rather shop. Even today, I avoid museums at all costs and cringe when visitors insist on dragging me to one. I recently had to inform one would-be museum-goer that unless the museum was having a sale on Capri pants, he would be going by himself.

But on this first trip to Paris there was no getting out of it. And that was fine; I deserved boredom and misery, welcomed it like an embrace. It was around this time that I started letting things hit me. I wanted to hurt myself, not badly, but enough to cause some discomfort. I was looking for something in the hair-shirt, scourge-belt range. These are harder to find than one might think, even in Paris, so I settled on more pedestrian weapons. I stood in the path of heavy swinging doors, letting the door smack me backward, savoring the weighty, satisfying thud. I dropped suitcases on my feet, slammed windows on my fingers, snapped branches back to hit me in the face.

I'm not sure why I bothered. Allowing myself to be photographed in Paris was masochistic enough. These are some of the most unattractive pictures ever taken of me. I am not particularly photogenic, but these were astounding, so bad and so funny that I felt I could not keep them to myself; when school started in the fall, I would present them to my French class. "Régardez-moi là. J'apparaît comme une banane corrompue, à fourrure et desséchée." There I am, sallow and pale, my dull, frizzy hair tamped down into a dowdy French braid (we were in France, after all), my eyes fluttering half-shut above a grim smile or a frown. There's my scary body, a twisting mobile of bones anchored by gunboat feet in protruding K-Swiss. The overall effect was clownish, Sideshow Bob in white jeans and a hair bow. "We're real glad we flew five thousand miles to get this wonderful picture of you beaming with contentment," Dad would say as he snapped the photo. "We're real glad we spent six thousand dollars to make you so happy."

But there were moments. There was the ten-dollar melon. Eating in France had been very, very difficult. Lunch was okay; there were salads, cold things, vegetable things that suited me well enough. But dinner was tough. I would have to slog my way through three full courses, each more contaminated than the last. I would finally find something I could eat, and it would arrive at the table garnished with a bug that had died en route from the kitchen. I would start to cry and out came the pills, then the liqueur, proffered by a solicitous proprietor; and then the pill and the alcohol would begin a little two-part harmony, and I would start to feel well enough to inspect my *macédoine de fruits* for blood spots.

The night of the melon we'd gone to a special, fancy restaurant. I was not pleased, as special and fancy usually meant pork in every course. I scanned the appetizer menu for the smallest, simplest thing. There it was, in tidy French cursive, in brown ink: a melon. Sixty francs. This seemed a little high, but perhaps it was a very special melon.

"You just ordered a ten-dollar melon," my father said as soon as the waitress walked away. My hand flew to my mouth and I felt guilt heat my face. I was, at this point, a very expensive child, what with the therapy and the drugs and the truckloads of paper towels, but these were incidentals, incurred but not intended. I did not ask for a car, did not demand expensive clothes or plead for electronics, did not request something indulgent simply because I wanted it. This I never did.

But then it came, and my gosh. What a perfect melon. It was small and cold, with smooth skin, striped dark green and light, like silk upholstery, and creamy orange flesh. I tasted it in my eyeballs. My gums sang for this melon. This melon could be prime minister. It could read minds, calm children, train pets, raise the dead. This was an extraordinary melon.

It was glorious. Normally I would not permit my family to come near my food, as they tended to contaminate it, but the melon made me generous. "Try it," I urged.

"That's a damn good melon," they agreed. "That melon is worth ten dollars, all right."

And so went the rest of our stay. There was my hand in a closing train door, and then the next day there were berries, perfect berries that made no demands and kept me perfectly happy for fifteen minutes. Then the French-English dictionary intentionally dropped on my foot, and then a movie, a really funny movie. There was the outburst, and then the pills. Things went this way and that, and then we were home.

Looking back on it now, I can't believe my parents put me on the plane in the first place. I was barely ambulatory and nearly catatonic. I was also extraordinarily unpleasant to be around. That's one thing when you're at home, but quite another when you're paying several hundred dollars a day to be somewhere else. None of us had all that much fun, and I'm sure my parents regretted their decision every time they had to pull me, chapped and barefoot, out of a fountain. But it ended up being the best thing they could have done. OCD is a disease of pathways. By taking me away, my parents plucked me out of the grooves I'd worn smooth with repeated rituals, compulsions, obsessions, and prayers. They took away my hiding places and touchstones.

When we got home I'd been up for thirty-six hours. I was exhausted and ambivalent and unsure of what to do next. Should I just go to sleep, or should I bathe, pray, vacuum and dust, then spend a couple hours checking all my books for unkosher food stains? I'd left a mantle; should I pick it up again? Reluctant but resigned, I decided yes, yes I should. It was such a comfortable mantle, such a flattering hair shirt, and I didn't have anything else to wear.

My mother found me in my bathroom, holding my nightgown by the hem to form an apron filled with water. I think I was worried an insect had touched it while I was gone.

"Don't," she said softly.

I thought for a minute, letting the water flow over the hem and all over the sink top. I knew she was right; this wasn't going to get me anywhere. But it had simply never occurred to me that I could do anything else.

Having an obsessive-compulsive impulse is like standing on red-hot coals. Every cell in your body is screaming for you to jump off. To keep standing there is so hard. It's just so hard. Leaning over the sink that night, I suddenly understood that that's what I had to do. I had to stand on the coals and take a tiny step forward. I had to feel the impulse and move past it. I got it, all of a sudden, just like that.

Maybe going away had given me some distance from my disease. Maybe, as I would soon write in my college application essays, *the trip to Europe had changed me forever.* Or maybe the years of checking sockets had paid off. Here, finally, was my lightbulb moment. I understood how I would get better. It was a fire walk, a circus feat, a high-wire balancing act of a thousand tiny steps. It would take ages, but all I had to do right now was turn off the faucet. Then tomorrow I would inch forward some more.

But right now, it was just the faucet, a simple twist to the right. "Okay," I told my mother, and turned the water off. I pulled the nightgown over my head. "Okay." I was so tired. I wadded the soggy flannel into a ball and offered it up. I was a tightrope walker charging forward, a flying Wallenda in damp underwear.

"For me?" my mother asked, holding the dripping gift at arm's length. "You shouldn't have."

"*De rien*," I answered. Then I shuffled to my bed, where I slept, and slept, and slept.

DISEASES I HAVE SELF-DIAGNOSED
(A PARTIAL LISTING)

1. Cancer (of breast, brain, uterus, kidneys, skin)
2. Hepatitis (A, B, and C)
3. Herpes (simplex I and II)
4. Toxic shock syndrome
5. AIDS (incl. attendant disorders of thrush and Kaposi's sarcoma)
6. Stroke
7. Deep vein thrombosis
8. Blood poisoning
9. Tuberculosis
10. Lupus
11. Schizophrenia
12. Parkinson's disease
13. Lou Gehrig's disease
14. Acid reflux disease
15. Congestive heart failure
16. Meningitis
17. Diabetes (I and II)
18. Lyme disease
19. Epstein-Barr virus
20. Tetanus
21. German measles
22. Diverticulitis
23. Retinitis pigmentosa

24. Leprosy
25. Necrotizing fasciitis
26. Multiple sclerosis
27. Vitiligo

Hell on Wheels

OR MAYBE IT was going to be harder than turning off a stupid faucet. Gah.

I was still a mess. The only difference was that I knew it. But that's something. If I wasn't on the road to recovery, at least I had a map.

My parents thought the road might be better traversed in a car. Shortly after we got back from Europe, they started badgering me about getting my driver's license. Driving would foster self-reliance and independence. It would also provide the means to run away, and should I be so inclined, my parents let me know they wouldn't try to hide the keys. I wasn't tempted. They'd tried to make me get my license a year earlier and it had not gone well at all.

Driving was not the first thing I was ever bad at. By age sixteen, I had proved myself inept at ballet, singing, and every sport except tetherball. I couldn't make gravy or plot a sine curve. But I had never failed at any task so spectacularly as when I tried to learn to drive. The fact that this was an activity that involved heavy machinery scared me to death. I mean, I couldn't pirouette, but you can't do much damage with a toe shoe.

If I had my way I would never have to drive at all. My plan was to make a lot of money doing something I was actually good at — the tetherball, maybe — and hire a chauffeur. Driving just didn't interest me at all. The only places I ever wanted to go were to the supermarket and the synagogue, and it wasn't like I was embarrassed to have my mother drive me there. The older married couples who made up the rest of the congregation didn't seem to think I was uncool just because my mom was my ride. No, I didn't need to learn to drive. I was fine.

My parents, however, had other ideas. "If you need to go out and pick up some more S.O.S. pads you can find your own damn ride," my mother sighed, putting her feet up on the coffee table and shaking open the newspaper. "I've shuttled you around enough today."

Our town was small but spread out, and you needed a car to get pretty much anywhere. By my sophomore year my parents were nearing their threshold. And even I could see that there would be some advantages to having a license. It would make getting to school much easier, for one. We lived too far away to walk, but my parents wouldn't drive me unless it was storming, and even then it had to be so bad that there was a very real possibility of being hit by lightning. Riding my bike was out of the question. Nothing was lamer than riding your bike to school. It would be better to arrive in a stroller. That was just as lame but not nearly as much work.

For a while I pedaled halfway there, hid my bike in my best friend's shrubs, and then walked the rest of the way with her. But this got to be too much of a production, and finally my parents started paying the student body president, who lived across the street, to drive me. The problem with that was that we had to leave at 6:00 a.m. We were in student government together and had a mandatory zero-period leadership class. I'd had quite enough of that. She couldn't resign, but I could, and I was looking to quit as soon as I found another ride.

So when my mother marched me down to the DMV the very day I was old enough to get my learner's permit, I dutifully complied. It was probably a bad sign that I had to cheat to pass the eye test. My mother thought I was faking when I struggled to make out the letters on the bigger rows, but I really couldn't see. Apparently my vision had gone to hell and I'd just been too busy inspecting the upholstery to notice. This explained why I wasn't doing so well in trigonometry, where I couldn't see the board, but not why I felt compelled to inspect that upholstery in the first place.

Well, at least I'd see the contaminants more clearly now. I was getting glasses, yet one more accessory to transform me from nerd into full-blown social outcast. What was the point of driving if I would have to wear glasses to do it? I was better off on my bike.

Once I had my permit and my corrective lenses I was ready for what my school called driver training and I called the most unpleasant experience of my life. Driver training is just an awful concept. It's *The Breakfast Club* crossed with *Speed*. Your life is in the hands of three people picked at random, with nothing to protect you but the passenger-side brake. Worse, you're unlikely to have a single shared interest. Personally, I like to have a little something in common with people when I'm going to be stuck in a car with them for four hours. I'd also like a little background. Are these the sort of people who drink gin for breakfast? Are they despondent over a recent breakup? Any past history of seizures? These are the sorts of things I want to know.

To be fair, my fellow trainees had more to fear from me than I did from them. At fifteen, they were all expert drivers, all of them capable of hot-wiring a Corvette or subbing for a demolition-driving brother should he become incapacitated after taking a round without a helmet. My only previous driving experience had been in a go-cart. It wasn't even a real go-cart. It was on a motorized track. You just sat in it and pretended to drive. I hadn't liked that one bit because I thought it made me look silly. Now, behind the wheel of a real car for the very first time, I felt the same way. I lurched through the town like a sitcom teen, my classmates providing the laugh track.

My mother was furious when I told her the teacher couldn't believe my parents had never let me drive before. "What do you mean, we should have been letting you drive?" she fumed. "It's illegal! The school told you I should have been letting you drive? Should I also be teaching you to shoot up and sniff glue?"

Four lessons later, I flunked driver training, surprising exactly no one.

Still stung by the teacher's reproach, my parents decided to continue my driving lessons themselves, in spite of the fact that we didn't have the specially equipped car or, for that matter, a beginner-friendly car of any kind. All three were stick-shift imports whose sensitive circuitry and hard-to-replace parts suggested they'd been designed to spite me and all the other stupid American teenagers. There was my father's sports car, which I was only allowed to ride in if I promised not to touch anything or to sweat on the upholstery. Out of the question. Then there was the battered VW Beetle my parents had bought on their honeymoon, now abandoned on the sidewalk in front of the house. Barely running, its sole responsibility now was to drive down the neighbors' property values. It was so dinged and dusty that my father's nurses had decorated it with surgical dressing and Band-Aids. Inside, the upholstery had dried and cracked into shards that poked your thighs, exposing tufts of horsehair and rusty springs. The condition they were in closely resembled that of the passenger seat in a friend's van we referred to as "the angry chair," because its errant springs had given more than one rider anal cysts. The unlucky shotgun passenger was forced to ride on his knees, facing in, with his backside resting on the dashboard.

So that was out, too. Thus it was decided that I would learn to drive on the family sedan, a Datsun Maxima that was annoying for a host of reasons. It was a talking car, which had seemed very novel when we first got it. If you did anything wrong — left a door ajar, forgot to turn off the lights, neglected to put on your seat belt — you were subjected to admonitions by the crisply reproachful voice system. Now, four years later, the novelty had worn off. "I took enough lip today," my mother barked when the electronic voice reminded her to release the hand brake, "and I'm not taking any more from you."

It was indeed a frustrating machine, a small car that seemed to have been designed for freakishly tall people. At five feet even,

I was just too little for it. The seat belt that should have crossed my chest crossed my throat instead, pressing uncomfortably on my windpipe. I couldn't see where the car began and ended. My parents bought me a booster, and I moved the seat as far up as it would go, but I still felt like a munchkin in a tank.

Was it just me? I had a friend who was a full foot shorter than I, only four feet tall, and she managed to get around just fine. There were people missing limbs and other crucial faculties, people who had to steer with their toes or teeth, all of whom could operate a car no sweat. At fifteen my sister could drive with just a knee, leaving her hands free to unwrap burritos and flip off tailgaters. But I *struggled*.

The problem, of course, was not in my body but in my brain. OCD is based upon an irrational belief that if you don't do something perfectly — wash your hands, pat the end table, plug in the coffeemaker the exact right way — someone will get hurt. But with driving, that's a distinct possibility. You're sitting in several thousand pounds of metal packing several gallons of flammable material. If you don't do something perfectly, someone really *might* get hurt.

Especially if I was at the wheel. Oh, I tried. My father and I dutifully set out for my driving lesson every Sunday. He felt it was important for me to master shifting gears before I was set loose in traffic, so our lessons took place in a deserted trucking company parking lot on the outskirts of town. I would drive around and around the lot for hours, shifting from first to second to third. This went on for months. My driving skills did not improve. My command of passive-aggression advanced considerably, however, as I shot my father hostile looks and made terse loaded comments. "You know, this would be *easier* for me if you weren't *scrutinizing* me so closely. *I* think I'm doing *fine.* I'm really not sure what you *expect.*"

My permit expired. My sixteenth birthday came and went. Instead of a car, I got a sewing machine. That was just as well. My anorexia was blazing again, and I was far too busy doing leg lifts to bother with the DMV. And since none of my clothes fit anymore, it was nice that I could take them in.

What did I need a license for, anyway? I didn't have anywhere to go. Of course, my classmates didn't either, and that didn't stop them. That was sort of the point, the aimless driving. They cruised. Cruising up and down the town's Main Street was such a popular activity the city council had tried to ban it, making it illegal to drive down the same street more than three times in an hour. But this only added to the appeal. Now you weren't just driving aimlessly; you were *breakin' the law.* The only time it was officially permitted was on Cruise Night, a summer festival featuring tricked-out funny cars, cover bands, and corn dogs. To commemorate the occasion, you could buy a T-shirt featuring a cat wearing sunglasses riding in a convertible.

I found the whole thing unspeakably tacky. Stupid cruising. Stupid cars. Stupid driver training. I was so turned off by the whole industry that I briefly considered using my post as president of Students Against Drunk Driving to undertake a new campaign, with a simpler, better acronym: Students Against Driving. Drink all you want, we would say, but lose the wheels. Sidecars, yes; cars, no.

I continued happily license-free for another year. Then we got back from Europe and my parents started badgering me again. Next summer I would turn eighteen, and they had less than a year of control over me left. If they didn't force me to get my license now they'd be stuck hauling me around forever.

In short order my mother made me renew my permit and announced that she would teach me to drive herself. This time there would be no laps around the parking lot. She put me right into traffic. "Sink or swim," she said, putting on her sunglasses and reclining the passenger seat.

Our first time out I plunged us into a ditch. Sink.

Next Sunday we tried again. This time, I cut off two cars and a tractor, but I managed to stay on the road. The following Sunday there was a near sideswiping, but that was all. I was gradually getting the hang of it.

A few months later I was competent enough to think about taking my driving test. But first I would have to pass driver training. Fortunately the instructor, who was also my Honors Chemistry instructor and the only teacher who knew my biweekly "dermatology" appointments were with a therapist, took pity on me and scheduled some sessions just for me, on his own time. Maybe it was just because he was so nice, or maybe he was afraid of pushing the dermatology patient too far when she had volatile Honors Chem supplies at her disposal. Whatever. I passed.

After all this trouble my actual DMV driving test was pretty uneventful. I got a 71, one point above failing, a D-minus. It was a fair grade. I was a D-minus driver. I got into an accident the very next day. It was so embarrassing. I had plenty of classmates who'd done that very thing, but they'd done it in the course of something wild and exciting, drag racing or stealing joyrides. I'd done it while taking two ten-year-olds to a matinee of *An American*

Tail. It was a really stupid accident, too, plowing into a parked car while doing a three-point turn. This would not have been so stupid if I hadn't been in a cul-de-sac at the time. Why a three-point turn? It was a *cul de sac!* Even the ten-year-olds couldn't help but laugh at me, and along with the singsongy complaints of the talking car itself, they formed a humiliating chorus.

Our Datsun was fine, but the Opel I'd smashed into now had a large canyon in the driver-side door. This was not a dent. You could bathe a toddler in this concavity. I carefully printed my name and phone number on a sheet of binder paper and left it under the windshield wiper. Then I drove to my father's office, handed his receptionist my license, went straight home, and obsessively cleaned the house until my parents arrived.

It was something, watching them try to convey the message that they were very, very angry with me, that I must never do this again, but that I shouldn't feel too discouraged to get right back behind the wheel tomorrow. As much as I wanted them to, they would not take away my driving privileges. Perhaps they should have. I promptly had two more accidents, neither one involving a moving car.

I'm not sure why I had so much trouble with stationary things, parked cars and traffic islands, curbs and poles. They were always jumping out at me, especially when I tried to park. In lots I would park away from all the other cars, in a remote corner where no one would ever think of parking next to me. A couple times, however, someone did, pulling in just as I was locking the car. "I think you should probably move your car, sir," I always told them. "I have no idea what I'm doing and I can pretty much guarantee I'll take out your rearview mirror."

Driving was hard, but parking was worse. I was lucky that we lived in a town with plenty of lots; I never had to parallel park, and fifteen years later, I still haven't, not once ever. But still, I struggled. The most difficult parking in town was in our own garage. It was small and narrow, and the driveway was angled, forcing you to come in from the side and then sharply maneuver straight, all the while being careful not to ding my father's sports car on the right or the side of the house on the left. There was no room for error, and my sister and I knocked mirrors off several times. Once my sister even knocked off a door. This turned out to be a blessing, however, because when we went to get that fixed, the mechanic noticed that the alignment was dangerously out of whack from my run-in with a curb several weeks earlier. I believe the phrase he used was *death trap*. We'd all been driving the car with no idea. "That could have killed any one of us," my mother said through gritted teeth, in the you-did-a-bad-thing-but-that's-*okay* tone that she was becoming expert at.

The thing was, I wasn't so bad if someone else was in the car. It was when I was alone, when there were no witnesses to verify that the curb had attacked *me*, that I got in trouble. When there was no one to distract me, my compulsions had full reign. Obsessive-compulsives vary in their habits, some of us praying and others pulling hair, but we all do the exact same thing when we get in a car: we circle endlessly, convinced that we ran someone over without noticing and then heading back to check. A normal person would know for sure if they'd committed a hit-and-run, but not me. "I don't remember goring that little girl at the stoplight, but I don't know, I can be forgetful that way," I would think. "Better go back and make sure." So I would circle back, and this time there would be an old man there, and half a block later I'd get to wondering if I'd hit him, and round and round we'd go. I could circle the block forever, in circuits that both mimicked and reinforced my neural loops. I was literally driving myself crazy. I was also in danger of being arrested for violating the anti-cruising ordinance.

Driving overwhelmed me. There were too many things competing for my attention. Besides fending off ruminations and looking for the bodies I couldn't remember hitting, there were a million other little things. I couldn't filter out the unimportant data. The song on the radio, the texture of the upholstery, the temperature inside the car, the state of my hair — all of these things were making equal demands on my attention. To have to deal with stop signs and other cars on top of everything else, and a clutch and a gearshift on top of *that*, was just too much.

The anorexia and scrupulosity allowed me at least the illusion of control, but in the car I had none. I'd felt that way before. Many years earlier we'd gone out for a Sunday morning drive in our egg-colored Corolla. A drunk plowed into us, scrambling it. Miraculously we were all fine, but the car was totaled. "Who the hell is drunk by eight a.m. on a Sunday morning?" my father wanted to know. No one in our family, certainly. The Jews didn't know how to party and the Catholics had the decency to wait until after mass.

I'd hated that feeling, of spinning helplessly in a vehicle I couldn't control. I felt that way every time I got behind the wheel now, spinning and spinning, my brain churning, the car circling the block yet one more time. I hated every errand I had to run, every trip to the post office or the library, and was amazed every time I arrived home intact. I never felt comfortable, and when I went off to college I was relieved that my parents gave me a computer instead of a convertible.

Over the next few years, I got better. The OCD subsided and I found I didn't mind driving as much. It helped that by then the family car was an automatic. My driving became automatic as well, and I was finally able to do everything I was supposed to without thinking too hard about it.

I don't drive very often now, but when I do, I do it fine. Over the years I have become perfectly competent, the only person I know with a spotless record. I've never gotten a ticket, not even for parking, though this may have something to do with the fact that I rarely drive and never park on the street.

When I did lose my license it was for fainting. I was on public transportation at the time, and woke up to find that the bus had stopped for a medical emergency. "Great," I said to the friend who was with me. "Now I'm going to be late for work." "*Really* late," my friend answered, pointing out that the emergency was me. This explained why I was lying on the floor. Apparently I'd passed out. It was a simple orthostatic faint; Yom Kippur had been the day before and I hadn't gotten fully rehydrated yet. But I went to the doctor just to make sure nothing was wrong. She informed me that by law she had to report my episode to the DMV and that I wouldn't be driving for a good long while.

I rarely drove, but this galled me. Losing my license for passing out? I had friends who'd kept their licenses after committing far worse infractions. It didn't seem fair. I knew someone who'd been apprehended driving drunk with a trunk full of stolen merchandise and gotten off with a warning. But I forget to drink enough water *one time* and I can't drive for a year? You couldn't lose your license for drinking, it seemed, but not drinking was another story.

In the end it worked out just fine. A year later I petitioned to have my license reinstated and got it back without too much trouble. I got a new picture, too, and it's the best picture I've ever taken. You should see it. I look like a model.

Now I'm legally clear to drive whenever I like. For the most part, however, I continue to live car-free, relying on public transportation and a network of indulgent driving friends. The qualities that made me a bad driver make me an excellent passenger, and I never have to look too far for a ride. I take care of all the details: picking a good radio station, modulating the heater or air conditioner, offering snacks and interesting banter. "Is everyone comfortable?" I ask. "Is everyone happy?" Then I angle back the seat, roll up the windows, and bask in the knowledge that this is one thing I'm *really* good at.

HELP JENNY GET TO HOMEROOM: A MAZE

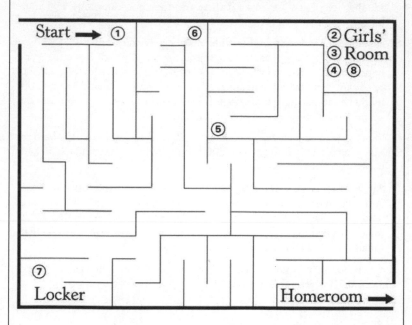

1. Head toward locker to retrieve calculus book. En route, accidentally brush against classmate. Pause. Is this classmate ritually unclean? What do you know about this classmate? Recall that she was sporting prominent hickeys earlier this year. Unclean. Head to girls' room to wash.

2. Wash hands for a count of one hundred and eighty Mississippis. On the way out, accidentally touch the door handle. Go back inside and wash three minutes more.

3. Proceed to locker. Realize you forgot paper towels you'll need to touch locker with. Return to girls' room.

4. Oh, look, there's Stacy Hibbs. You heard she'll do anything for a six pack. Look at how she's dressed — it's probably true. Stop thinking bad things. Stop thinking bad things. Is this gossip? Mental gossip? Thinking awful things like this? It probably is. It is. You are going straight to hell. Okay. You have to do a good deed to make up for this. Here's what you'll do: you'll stay in the girls' room until someone comes in, then you will pay this

person a compliment. It has to be a sincere compliment or it will be a lie. If you lie, you will have to pay two sincere compliments to make up for the lie plus one compliment for the bad thought in the first place. Three is a good number. Yes. Let's just make it three and then you can go back to your locker.

5. Head toward locker again. En route, make eye contact with Social Studies teacher. Wait. Was eye contact appropriately friendly and respectful? Perhaps it wasn't. Perhaps it somehow conveyed disrespect for your elders. Spend five minutes contemplating whether or not you should go find said teacher and make some other friendly and respectful gesture to compensate for possibly sinful look you gave her earlier.

6. What's that you just stepped on? Is that blood? Is that *blood?* It's hard to say — an old brownish stain — but it could be blood. Go find a hose and wash your shoes.

7. Arrive at locker. Open locker using paper towel. Retrieve calculus book and place in backpack, being careful not to let it touch your lunch, because who knows where that book has been. Approach trash can to dispose of towel. While throwing it away, accidentally touch the part of the towel that touched the locker handle. Return to girls' room to wash.

8. The bell rang five minutes ago. You are so late. Tardiness is a sin, it's a sin, and you'll never be able to wash it off.

Shalom Bayit

So MY FAMILY was having its first real Shabbat dinner and this was not how it was supposed to go at all. For starters, my father was supposed to be wearing pants. This was my very special Shabbat dinner and here he was wearing swim trunks. Though I'd laid white dresses on their beds, my mother had opted for sweats and my sister for obscenely tight ankle-zip jeans and a hot pink tank top. Because it was a special occasion, she'd accessorized with large rhinestone hoops, fingerless gloves, and, on her shoulder, a chip the size of a small microwave.

This was not how it was supposed to go at all. We were supposed to be wearing matching formalwear and shy, beatific smiles. I had it all planned out. My mother and sister and I would light the Shabbat candles, and then my parents would recite the traditional blessing of the children. I didn't know the Hebrew formula, but I figured we could just make something up. *"Hava nagila shalom aleichem tova feldshuh,"* our parents would chant solemnly, laying their hands on our heads. They would shut their eyes in concentration, and their voices would build to a fervent wail. "May you rise up like the bread of the earth. May your lives be as sweet as fruit of the vine, blessed fruit of our loins."

Then my father would make the blessings over the wine and the challah, and we'd sit down to the delicious kosher meal I'd spent all day preparing. There would be course after course and the dinner would last late into the night. When we could finally eat no more, we'd put down our forks and join hands to sing the blessing after meals and a few of our favorite Hebrew folk songs. By now we would all be tired, but we'd be having too much fun to stop. "Just one more song, Papa," we'd plead, "and then we'll go to bed." My father would pretend to be stern, shaking his head, but then he would chuckle and nod and lead us all in "Tzur Mishelo."

Instead he was distractedly humming the theme to *Dirty Harry.* The lugubrious tune suited the doleful, uneasy mood of the dinner. We'd gotten off to a bad start when I'd insisted on making kiddush, the blessing over the wine. My warbly, halting Hebrew and fervent delivery had embarrassed everyone, including me. Then came the food, each dish more weirdly inedible than the last. It was hard not to view these concoctions as open expressions of high-fiber hostility. Oh, I'd tried to make something nice. I'd combed through cookbooks for days, looking for recipes that were both low-calorie and contaminant-free. In the end I'd settled on coleslaw dressed in apple cider vinegar and Sweet'n Low; V-8 gazpacho; quiche made from skim milk, egg whites, and Mrs. Dash; and a salad of dried fruit. What the menu lacked in flavor it made up in laxative properties. These dishes had the volatility of Semtex. Had I simply handed my family boxes of Feen-a-Mint, I could have achieved the same result with far less work. It was terrible.

I tried to make conversation, tried to put a positive spin on things. "I bet you didn't know there's more fat in the gazpacho than in the quiche," I chirped. "I read today that fresh apples can give you cancer, so it's a good thing we're having dried." Unable to say anything nice, my family said nothing at all. Now we sat uncomfortably, shooting one another loaded looks as we absently played with our food, bulldozing our prunes into the quivery, anemic quiche.

By 6:45 my sister was clearing her plate. "Can I go now?" she demanded. "You said all I had to do was show up for Jenny's stupid dinner. You didn't say anything about hanging around all night." When my parents didn't offer a protest she snatched the car keys and charged out the door. My father wandered off to watch *Washington Week in Review*, my mother went to her sewing room, and I retreated to the living room to stretch out on the Oriental rug and pitch a fit.

The dinner had been my therapist's idea. She'd thought it would be good for me to include my family in my religious activities. This was part of my rehabilitation plan. We had a *plan*. I was seventeen now, and all parties agreed it was finally time to get my craziness under control, while my parents could still make me and before I would face long prison terms should my compulsions run afoul of the law. So now there was a plan, with professionals, medication, contracted behavior, and consequences.

The rehabilitation process would be guided by the Jewish principle of *shalom bayit* — "peace in the home." The idea was that I would modify my religious practice to keep my family happy, and they would try to accept a ritual or two in return. I'd retained enough bat mitzvah Hebrew to understand that the phrase also meant "goodbye, home," and the threat was implicit. If I didn't shape up, I would be shipped out.

I knew it wouldn't take much. My mother liked to leave out brochures from military schools, convents, and wilderness challenge programs to remind me how thin the ice beneath my feet actually was. My family had had it with me. All teenagers are problematic, but I was problematic in a spectacularly tedious way. Binge drinking, promiscuity, delinquency, paint huffing — all of these things have their fun moments for the family that has to deal with them. My sister's occasional partying was a good time for us all. She was a fun drunk, and in that lovely twilight between getting caught and getting grounded, she was oblivious and effusive, working the room like a cabaret singer. "Oh, *hellooooo*, everyone. What a good-looking crowd. Anyone here from Sacramento?"

But a religious compulsion was as dull as it was annoying. It didn't even give my parents the satisfaction of righteous indignation. *I* was holier than *thou*. That was the whole point. And a Jewish religious compulsion was worst of all. Truth be told, they rather enjoyed our Jesus-freak acquaintances, with their colorful stories and lively turns of phrase. They were fun company, quick to offer pamphlets that were useful for jotting down phone numbers or wrapping your gum in. All I could provide was dour approbation and antibacterial Handi Wipes.

But now we had a counselor and a therapeutic plan to make me better. The first step would be to distinguish normal Jewish practice from crazy compulsive behavior. Because the therapist was not Jewish, she suggested we consult a rabbi as well. It would be his job to draw the line between the weird religious behavior I made up and the weird religious behavior Judaism actually requires.

By now our synagogue had hired a new rabbi, so we made an appointment to meet him and explain our situation. I'd liked the previous rabbi very much, but she knew better than to trust me. This new one, however, was a blank slate. Perhaps he would recognize that I was not, as everyone said, completely off my nut, that I was just especially devoted. I had hopes.

It took him about five minutes to figure out I was crazy. He was a reasonably patient man, but he soon learned to set his jaw and rub his brow when he saw me coming. This would be a challenge, teaching me to be a normal Jew. My religious observance was just *off*. Because I'd been practicing mostly in isolation, my practice was like that of a long-lost tribe, like those Chinese or Indian Jews who avoided pork and wore funny hats but didn't remember why. It looked familiar, but it wasn't quite right. I prayed three times a day but said strange prayers I made up myself. I separated milk and meat not just in the kitchen, but in the bathroom as well. Sometimes I wore yarmulkes, and sometimes I wore Kleenex.

Over the next few months the rabbi tried to set me straight. I had no obligation to pray three times a day, he told me, but if

I was going to do it, I might as well do it right. He taught me the proper prayers and made me cut the calisthenics portion of my service. While it was customary to keep separate plates for meat and milk, he explained, to keep separate toothbrushes, trash cans, and toilets was not. I had no obligation to cover my head, but if I insisted, a lace doily would be more appropriate than a paper towel. I did not always believe him and sometimes continued to insist on doing things my way, but mostly I deferred.

The rest of it we worked out in counseling. Because OCD hadn't yet been recognized as a fairly straightforward chemical disorder, my treatment included family therapy sessions and a fair amount of blaming my parents. Every few weeks, my family would come to my appointment, sitting stone-faced and sullen on the leather couches while I fired accusations at them. "Maybe I wash my hands so much because you spanked me that one time," I suggested. "Maybe I don't eat because Vicky used to spit in my food. Maybe I pray all the time because you wouldn't let us get cable and I have nothing better to do."

It was like trying to make a cat feel guilty. They had nothing to feel sorry about, except maybe the part about the cable — that really wasn't fair. But other than that they'd been great. Psychiatry may not yet have known that my family wasn't to blame, but my family sure did. As far as they were concerned, family therapy was a colossal waste of time and money, not to mention a huge embarrassment. "There's nothing wrong with counseling," we said, but of course there was. Counseling was for crazy people. Wasn't that the whole idea?

That we were seeing a therapist in my father's own practice, a colleague, just made it that much more uncomfortable. To make matters worse, Psychiatry and OB/GYN shared an office. Either way, if anyone saw us all trooping in, it was clear that the Traigs were *in trouble*. We would have been better off working out our family hostilities with hunting accidents, like our neighbors did. "Shalom bayit," said through gritted teeth, became the family mantra.

This kind of therapy shouldn't have worked but it did. I don't know. I was starting to get a little better. By October I could sit on the recliner without lining it with paper towels first. I could read the newspaper without cutting it into ribbons, could watch a movie without praying, could eat without plastic bags on my hands. In my naked, wobbly way, I was getting on track. I remember spending this year feeling like an infant, like a stroke victim learning to walk and eat and breathe again. I had to learn to do everything over. How did you sit down to a meal without inspecting the dishes first? How did you walk without pausing to contemplate your sins? How did you sit without rocking? How did you hold a conversation without trying to anoint your companion's forehead?

It was going to be a long year. I was getting better, but for every three taps forward, there were two taps and a shoulder tic back, especially where socialization was concerned. On my own, I was okay, or getting there, but put me in a group and I was weird, weird, weird.

At the time I was tutoring a popular classmate who'd suffered some minor brain damage when she fell asleep at the wheel and crashed into a tree. Now she was having trouble with basic math and vocabulary, and it was my job to make sure she could add in time for the SATs. Misty struggled with two plus two, but her social skills were completely intact. I marveled at her ability to flirt and charm, skills that I lacked utterly. Being in the in-crowd, or being in any crowd at all — it was just beyond me. But Misty had it down. When she talked to you, you felt as though you were the most special person in the world. When you talked to me, you felt as though you were competing with the mental transistor feed that held most of my attention. If she plucked a loose thread off your sweater, as I often felt compelled to, you felt lucky she noticed. With me you just felt scared that I might proceed to strip-mine your cardigan for hairs and other impurities.

Even though there was a shaved patch underneath the picture hat Misty somehow managed to pull off, she seemed to be doing so much better than I was. Even with her cane and limp, she was still the most popular girl in school. She was the one with brain damage, but I was the one who couldn't go to a party without my own roll of paper towels and can opener. I was the one who couldn't take PE because aerobics posed too many moral dilemmas.

This was not the senior year I'd imagined. I'd planned to be the president of every club and the star of every musical. I knew that MVP was probably out of reach, since I didn't play any sports, but I thought an award for "Most Spirited" was a strong possibility. "Most Likely to Succeed" was a lock. I'd have a boyfriend and we'd be voted "Cutest Couple." We would also receive individual awards for "Best Smile" and "Prettiest Eyes," as well as "Best Diction" and "Cleanest Shoes."

This would be the year I reaped the rewards for serving dutifully on every committee, decorating the gym for every stupid dance and rally for the past three years. Come spring, my picture would be on every page of the yearbook. There would be candids of me playfully soaping cars at fund-raising car washes, rehearsing my big solo, studying thoughtfully on the quad. It would be so over the top that I'd be embarrassed, and would grow bashful and shy when asked to sign it. "I don't know why they put so many pictures of me in here," I'd say, uncapping my ballpoint. "I feel like the school mascot. Which, in a way, I guess I am."

When the yearbook finally came out in May it was testament to my utter lameness. My sole candid showed me playing with stuffed animals at a toy drive I'd organized, holding an oversized teddy bear aloft with a tight smile on my face. The "Sad Toys for Sad Tots" campaign was my one success that year. I'd quit Student Council and Drama Club to devote myself entirely to charity drives and a series of ill-conceived volunteer schemes. The two most notable flops had been my "Third World Luncheon" fund-raiser, at which I charged five dollars for bread and water, or would have, had even one person attended; and my "D-D-D-Don't Drink and Drive!" rap song, broadcast over the PA system to the entire student body. I'd recorded it without a microphone into a Fisher-Price cassette deck, and the poor sound quality was the only thing that kept me from having to drop out of school the next day. It was so scratchy and quiet you couldn't tell it was me, or that I was saying, ". . . And th-th-th-that ain't cool!"

But there were steps forward. There were signs that I was getting better. I could wear leather shoes without feeling compelled to avoid dairy afterward. I could take out the trash without changing into a plastic smock first. I could watch television. I could get through a book.

By early winter my parents trusted me enough to leave me alone with my sister for a week. I don't know which one of us was more nervous. I was afraid my sister was going to host nightly keggers. My sister was afraid I was going to fumigate. "No parties. No steam-cleaning," my parents said, throwing their suitcases into the car. "You'll be fine. You'll be *fine*."

The first day of their trip I came home from school to find the bloated body of the family dog floating facedown in the pool. We were off to quite a start. I'd spent the past five years flipping out every time I'd found a dead bug in the water. To find a fur-bearing member of the family was too much.

But I didn't lose it, not completely. I ruminated for fifteen minutes or so, wondering if it was worse to do nothing or to jump in and attempt mouth-to-mouth, thereby contaminating myself. My sister decided for me. "He's been dead for hours, and you're wearing wool," she said. It couldn't be helped. The dog was epileptic, and we figured he'd probably fallen in the pool during a seizure.

I missed him terribly, but his death did make things a little simpler, as many of my compulsions had revolved around his care. Of course, I could never go in the pool again now, but that was fine, too, as many of my other compulsions revolved around fishing things out. Vicky called someone to come get the body, and a few more people to come over for refreshments, and I retreated to my room to pray and write some lists.

And so went the rest of the week, my sister hosting nightly get-togethers while I cleaned my desk accessories. I felt a little uneasy, but when I came downstairs to get the bleach I was perfectly polite to everyone. If nothing else, the week had proved that I could, finally, act somewhat normal in mixed company for whole minutes at a time.

Now that I could be around other people without trying to wash their feet, my therapist thought it was time for me to start socializing with people my age again. Up until now my social contact had been limited mostly to the hour I spent each week at synagogue, sharing pleasantries with the older married couples who were the only other regulars. That was fine with me. They were warm and congenial, and they shared my interest in butter cookies, dried apricots, and yarn. We had plenty to talk about.

But now my therapist thought it was time for me to be among peers. We would start small, with a Jewish youth group. The synagogue youth group proved very small indeed, both in size and in age level. Apparently I was the only person over age eleven who was still the least bit interested in religion. Everyone else had bailed as soon as the bar mitzvahs were over, having realized that never again would they get gift certificates and savings bonds for going to temple. Undeterred, I continued to attend, spending every Sunday night eating graham crackers with sixth-graders while we discussed Jewish themes in the works of Judy Blume.

I have always been terribly immature, but even I knew I was too old for this. I was short, but I couldn't pass for a preteen and I looked freakishly out of place. In the pageant, they had to obscure my face. I played the rear end of a dancing golden calf. The head was ten.

Eventually we managed to find another Jewish youth group several counties over. It was a branch of a stridently Zionist organization whose sole purpose was to encourage emigration to Israel. I dutifully went to meetings, driving three hours for hourlong gatherings at which we learned about the Balfour Declaration and ate falafel. The other kids were mostly the American-born children of Israelis, who were skilled at tanning and making fun of their parents' accents. I liked them quite a bit but was afraid we didn't have much in common, as I was only interested in emigrating to Israel if the Messiah was my travel agent. I mean, I wanted to go to the Promised Land, but there was no way I was going to leave my farm town just to end up on a kibbutz.

Also, they camped. They were always holding forest Shabbatons and redwoods retreats. I didn't understand that at all. The way I saw it, after spending forty years in the wilderness, Jews had pretty much done their time. Why should we get sunburned and bug-bitten now?

"Fresh air and open sky," my mother said, tossing my jeans into a duffel bag, when the youth group announced the next Shabbat on the Swamp. "It will do you good, and do me even better. I need a couple days off."

I wasn't so sure. *Shalom bayit* was supposed to be our guiding principle. "Shalom *house*," not "shalom tent." Not "shalom sleeping bag." But there would be kosher hot dogs, and my parents had been adamant, so I acquiesced.

This was maybe a bad idea. This was maybe a little more than I could handle at this point. It had only been a couple months since I'd stopped wearing surgical masks around the house. I ended up spending the better part of the weekend rocking back and forth by the campfire, ruminating on Talmudic matters and keeping a close eye on the embers. I left my post only to pester the youth group leader with obscure theological inquiries.

I tended to do this whenever I encountered an adult who seemed at all knowledgeable about Judaism. There was my rabbi, but I'd worn him out already. So now I kept lists of things to ask and would let fly with a litany of inquiries whenever I encoun-tered a potential resource. There was just so much I needed to know, now that I was trying to live a normal Jewish life. But be-cause my knowledge of Judaism came from a half-baked assort-ment of dubious sources, my questions did, too. They had the logic of a sentence translated from English to Spanish and back again. All I'd wanted to know was which prayers to say before bed and which ones to say before eating, but the words came out funny and convoluted, like I'd asked "How does it say the tradi-tional prayer of the hour to be put to bed?" or "Does it has to say you a benediction on the water?" They were words, but they didn't necessarily make any sense. I didn't have any context, didn't know how to phrase things correctly.

When the youth group leader told us we should feel free to ask him questions, I don't think mine were what he had in mind. "I don't think you understand," he told me. "I'm a Near East Studies grad student, not a rabbi. I can answer any questions you may have about Moshe Dayan, but I'm afraid I just don't know if dirt is kosher."

Everyone was friendly and kind, but it was still more than I could handle. I could act normal for a few hours at a stretch but two whole days was just too much. I came home exhausted and spent, feeling just as burned as the charcoal briquette I smelled like. I was getting better, but there were still some things, like peeing outside, that I just wasn't ready for.

Well, at least it had been nice to spend a couple days around people who looked like me. My school consisted almost entirely of blonds and Latinos, and I often felt like a small Semitic alien, like an ALF puppet who'd accidentally wandered onto the set of a

Mexican soap opera. Years later, when I was at Brandeis, it would be the first time I lived among people who looked just like me. Everyone was five feet tall with glasses and curly brown hair. It was unsettling, and for the first time in my life I considered dating outside my faith.

But in high school my looks were just one more way I was different from everyone else. I had no peers. What teenager spends her free time reading psalms and sterilizing salad tongs? These are activities you do alone. There are no washing societies, no burnt-offering clubs. My rabbi had told me there were other kids like me, but I was pretty sure he was lying. I knew I was the weirdest kid in the world. It was obvious.

I was weird not just because I was crazy, but because I was religious at all. For my friends, it would all amount to the same thing anyway. Orthodox Judaism was just as foreign to them as OCD was. It was just too hard to explain why I couldn't go out Friday night, why I couldn't go to McDonald's, why I would not be wearing the new off-the-shoulder look. It was easier just to lie: I was grounded, I was dieting, I had acne on my upper back.

Why would they understand? Even to Jews, I looked crazy. I knew so few, and the handful I met didn't seem to share my fascination with the minutiae of usury laws. I was speechless when my parents finally dug up someone who did. The college-age daughter of some family friends had become Orthodox, and my parents asked her to come talk to me.

"You can ask me anything," she said over Baskin-Robbins cones she assured me were kosher, but for once I was too overwhelmed to form a question. She was the first Orthodox person I'd ever met and I was fascinated by her. So this was what an Orthodox girl looked like. I scrutinized her every aspect. "Orthodox shoes," I thought, examining her sandals. "Orthodox watch, Orthodox cardigan, Orthodox barrette." What amazed me most was that she looked completely normal. I'd expected someone from another planet entirely, with accessories I'd never seen before, things with foreign names like *yechsmatas* and *tchabainiks*. But she looked just like me, only taller and with better hair. She was a revelation, living proof that I could be both sane and practicing, and that I would look better without bangs.

I could ask her anything? I wanted to ask if I could come live with her. I longed to be her ward, but I doubted that college dorms smiled on sophomores taking in seventeen-year-old adoptees. Besides, I didn't think I could handle the coed bathrooms.

In the meantime I was supposed to be spending more time with my school friends. I liked them, but seeing them was still a lot of work, as it required me to act normal for long stretches of time. I was trying, though. I was trying so hard. I even tried to put a positive spin on the fact that I was completely incapable of attending my own prom, the strapless gown and the sheer hose being just unthinkable, not to mention the champagne and the boy with *his needs*. It was out of the question. But stay home and sulk? Not me! I was trying, trying, trying. "I know Kevin wants to go with me, but I think it would be hypocritical for me to go, since I think proms are so lame," I told my friends. "Let's all boycott and I'll host an antiprom dinner party instead. We'll call it a 'Morp' and we'll wear 'creative formal' and drink sparkling cider."

This, too, had been my therapist's idea. It wasn't quite the social event of the season. The guests included the drum major, an Amway representative, and the only girl at school who was in my height percentile, just out of a wheelchair after the procedure that would make her several inches taller. They were my friends and I certainly liked them, but there was little chance any of us was going to be crowned prom queen.

Because I'd learned nothing at all from the apocalyptically fibrous Shabbat dinner I'd made my family several months earlier, I served the exact same thing with exponentially worse results. I don't know if it was the underdone quiche or the haphazardly prepared gazpacho, but something made me and several unlucky guests catastrophically sick. We hadn't even gotten to our dried fruit before they began folding over in their seats. "Cramps," they exhaled painfully, before leaping over one another to get to the bathroom.

This was not what I'd planned for the entertainment portion of the evening. I'd optimistically rented *Girls Just Wanna Have Fun*, the feel-good romp in which Sarah Jessica Parker and Helen Hunt triumph over disapproval and *dance*, but there was no point in watching it now. We'd just have to keep pausing it while guests scurried off to answer the colonic demands of the offending microbe. And thus we got to spend our prom night like the rest of our classmates, bent over a toilet.

So in my own strange way I was fitting in. And while I was treated to many reruns of the meal, as it came up and out again and again, it was not, otherwise, a repeat of that first Shabbat dinner I'd served months before. Things had changed. Here one of my worst obsessive fears had come true: I had served my friends contaminated food. The world didn't end, and afterward, I didn't feel compelled to pull out my hair and then burn it as a restitution offering. I actually felt pretty good. Oh, sure, I was nauseous and crampy, but as we sat there together clutching our abdomens, I felt, for the first time in a long while, as if I was part of something.

Judaism is always calling for the separation of kinds: meat from milk, male from female, linen from wool, this seed from that, and this may have been a lesson I learned too well. I could dissect and detach anything. It was the blending that I had trouble with. It was the integration I couldn't do. When I found myself in big Jewish communities, at Brandeis or in Israel, I became less religious, stopped going to shul, spent Saturdays by myself in bed, reading tabloids and eating Danish. I was so used to practicing by myself that it would take me a long time to learn to practice in a community.

Shalom can mean goodbye, but it can also mean hello; *bayit* can also mean community. That's what I'd been struggling to get. That's what this year had been, really, a process of learning to integrate, to come into line with normal Jewish practice, so I could pass for normal, stay in school, rejoin society at large. By June, I wasn't completely socially normal, but I was getting close. I could attend my graduation. Afterward, my parents had a party, and I could eat the food even though it was in communal dishes. I could shake the guests' hands without a napkin in my palm.

I was, in fact, getting downright grabby. As I neared sanity my family was horrified to discover that the by-product of my rehabilitation was the open expression of affection and sincerity. I'd always had a smart mouth, but now, suddenly, I was given to saying things like, "You know, Vicky, it's okay to *feel.*" We'd be in the middle of dinner and out of nowhere I'd announce, "I can hear my heart beating. Isn't that an amazing thing? All on its own, it's just beating, keeping me alive. The human body is truly a wondrous thing. I just wanted to share that thought with you." At the mall, I'd accost my sister over the sale rack with a mock pouty face, demanding a hug. "I don't mind if you want to wash my sneakers or sanitize my purse," she hissed, "but there's no way in hell I'm letting you *snuggle*."

So this is what a year of therapy had bought us. I was functional but incredibly annoying. Well, at least the timing was good. In three months I would leave for nearby UC Berkeley, and my family couldn't wait.

Personally I was a little nervous about it. I spent all summer preparing myself, agonizing over which habits I could take with me and which ones would have to stay home. I would have two roommates, who, I imagined, would be put off by someone who spent three hours a day rocking on a chair in the center of the room, whispering prayers. While they might not mind if I sanitized my room keys, they probably wouldn't like it if I did the same to theirs. They wouldn't know what to make of my unusual headwear, my cleaning products, my need to keep things off the floor.

Well, then, I'd just have to act normal.

By August I was pretty sure I could. The morning I was to leave, I perched on my torturously uncomfortable prayer chair and said my devotions for what I knew would be the last time. I prayed for a good year, nice roommates, decent grades, and frizz control. Then I finished packing up my things, taking two prayer books but not my makeshift yarmulke, my shampoo but not my antibacterial bleach spray, my calculus notes but not my collection of lists. I was ready. We loaded up the car and we were on our way, and I only made us turn back once to check the outlets. Alone in the house, I said goodbye to the walls and floors, my hiding spots and sanctuaries. Goodbye, goodbye. *Shalom, bayit.*

Three hours later I was all moved in to my new room. I would have to share the phone and the closet, but the southwest corner was all my own. I could set it up any way I wanted. If I wanted to spread a tarp over my bunk, well, that was my decision. If I needed to align my books by height, I was free to do so. Mostly, however, I just worried about aesthetics. Did the Klimt look better over the bed or over the desk? What did the Monet print say about me? Did it convey my sophistication and sensitivity? Or would I be better off with the Matisse?

After several hours of ordering my father around, not there but *there,* things were just the way I wanted them. My parents left, and it was perfect. There had been some discussion of trying to find a new counselor at school, to ease the transition and prevent a relapse, but as soon as my parents said goodbye I realized I wouldn't need one. I'd expected to feel scared, or at least wistful. Instead I felt fantastic, so good I wanted to jump on the bed, so good I didn't care if my shoes rendered the bedspread unclean. I could wash it a hundred times if I wanted to, or throw it away, or not worry about it at all.

I wasn't worried. I could make any decision I wanted now. I would make some bad ones — it's a fact that I ate Raisin Bran for every meal that first year — but on the whole I did pretty well. I passed all my classes, made friends, fit in. Nobody at college knew how crazy I'd been, and they treated me as if I was perfectly normal. Maybe I was. I kept waiting for the scrupulous impulses to come back, but they didn't. I did just fine.

Now my parents were in the parking lot. I waved goodbye out the window, shalom, shalom. This was great. I could do *anything*. I could join a cult. I could follow the Dead. I could grow out my bangs. I could take up drumming. I could learn Chinese. I could become an anarchist or a vegan. I could stop wearing socks. I could run down the hallway and touch every doorknob. I could stay out, sleep late, run away, run back. I could do anything. Shalom.

Acknowledgments

Thanks first and most to my family, for putting up with me then and letting me write about it now. They are charming, lovely, wonderful people, and if they don't appear so herein this is only further proof of what they have had to endure from me. Trust me: every one of them is a peach. Thanks, too, to the rest of the tree: the Zweimans, the Clabbys (especially Mary Lou), the Neffs (especially Maureen), the Schleichers (especially wise and helpful Miriam), and the McGraths, Peter McGrath most of all, for being such a generous reader and patient hand-holder. Thanks to the following people for encouragement and advice: Dave Kneebone, Gideon Lewis-Kraus, Dave Eggers, Vendela Vida, Amie Nenninger, Matthue Roth, Mikyla Bruder, Ryan Gray, Wendy Hillis, Claudia Ocampo, Suzi Ishikawa, Ned Newcomer, and the angelically supportive Angela Hernandez. Thanks to crackerjack agents Emily Forland and Wendy Weil. Thanks to whip-smart editor Reagan Arthur, who has the ace literary sensibilities befitting her wonderfully authorial name. Thanks to her equally smart assistant, Michael Mezzo, and to Betsy Uhrig and all the other quick minds at Little, Brown, especially Michael Pietsch. Yeesh. What a great bunch of people. I'm lucky to know you all.

About the Author

J ENNIFER T RAIG writes for the *Forward* and McSweeney's Internet Tendency, and has coauthored a number of illustrated books published by Chronicle.

READING GROUP GUIDE

Devil in the Details
Scenes from an Obsessive Girlhood

by Jennifer Traig

My Personal Food Handler's Licensing Exam
by Jennifer Traig

Encourage members of your reading group to take the test.

1. Food should be stored:
   a. Below 60 degrees Fahrenheit.
   b. Below 40 degrees Fahrenheit.
   c. In alphabetical order from left to right.

2. If you find an insect in the produce, you should:
   a. Throw it away.
   b. Rinse produce thoroughly and cut away affected part, then serve.
   c. Rinse produce thoroughly and cut away affected part. Decide produce still carries the taint of death and throw it away, but not in the kitchen garbage can. Use the garbage in the garage instead. Wash your hands well, tap the counter three times to ward off death, then say your afternoon prayers.

3. Serving utensils should be:
   a. Stored in ice water.
   b. Flash-sterilized in the dishwasher.
   c. Anointed in the Jacuzzi.

4. An acceptable salad dressing is:

   a. Oil and vinegar.

   b. Herbed aioli.

   c. Tap water.

5. The black specks in the vegetable soup are probably:

   a. Pepper.

   b. Poppy seeds.

   c. Dead insects. They are totally, totally dead insects. Go wash
   the bowl until your hands bleed.

6. If food is dropped on the floor, you must:

   a. Wash it before serving.

   b. Throw it away.

   c. That depends. Where did you drop it, exactly? On the carpet? If it was on the carpet you should throw it away and go
   wash your hands. But if it was on the linoleum, where you
   saw bacon grease drip that one time, you're going to have to
   throw it away, wash your hands, then wash everything you're
   wearing. Shower and change into a noncontaminated outfit.
   This outfit will instantly become contaminated because it
   takes more than one shower to remove the taint of bacon.
   Shower again. Change into another noncontaminated outfit,
   and avoid the kitchen for the rest of the week.

True or False:

1. Toothpaste has calories. T F

2. Air can be unkosher. T F

3. Salmonella can flourish in the balmy climes of hell. T F

QUESTIONS AND TOPICS FOR DISCUSSION

1. The author writes, "There's a fine line between piety and wack-ass obsession." When does religious observance become religious obsession? What's the difference between clinical scrupulosity and simple devotion? Why is it okay, say, to pre-tear toilet paper for the Sabbath, as Orthodox Jews do, but crazy to cut religious references out of the newspaper?

2. Of all the biblical laws, Jennifer becomes obsessed with some strange ones, like those surrounding agriculture, livestock, and ritual impurity. Why these? If you had OCD, what might you be obsessed with?

3. The author describes OCD triggers: "Cross-culturally and transhistorically, we zero in on the exact same things: details and doorknobs, electrical sockets, light switches, blood, bugs, and germs." What do you think draws obsessive-compulsives to these particular items?

4. Since the 1980s, there's been much progress in understanding OCD as a chemical disorder, but it's still not fully understood. What do you suspect causes it? Is it all nature, or partly nurture?

5. Jennifer's family dealt with her scrupulosity with humor. Do you think that was the right thing to do? How would you have dealt with it?

6. Discuss the ways in which Jennifer's religious issues were compounded by growing up in an interfaith family. And how were they compounded by her growing up in such a small Jewish community?

7. The author writes, "There is a magic in OCD, revolving as it does around lucky numbers, magic words, formulas, and rituals." What is its magic? What's the difference between OCD and superstition?

8. The author offers several anthropological analyses of anorexia: it's an attempt to be perfect, a response to the media, an effort to delay puberty, a guilty response to having too much, a rite of passage among the upper middle class. Do you think any of these explanations is accurate?

9. Jennifer Traig takes a light approach to a serious issue. Do you think it's wrong to make light of mental illness? Discuss the ways in which the author uses humor.

10. Who was your favorite character in *Devil in the Details*? With whom did you identify most?

11. As adolescents, Jennifer and her sister have a complicated relationship. Jennifer writes, "It has always seemed strange to me that so few siblings in the Bible get along. . . . Biblical family reunions require flocks of she-goats and wrestling matches; they end in false accusations and hard truces made over fathers' graves. The best you can hope for is the family diplomacy employed by Abraham and Lot: you go right, and I'll go left." What do you make of this?

A SPECIAL READING GROUP ACTIVITY

Make everyone in your book club uncomfortable by sharing the answers to these overly personal questions!

1. Confess the craziest thing you've ever done. Not crazy like "wild and crazy." Crazy like institutionalized.

2. At one point, Jennifer's parents make her sign a contract listing the embarrassing revelations that will be shared with her friends if she doesn't shape up. What embarrassing revelations would your parents put on your contract?

3. Although Jennifer's specific condition is relatively rare, the mortifications of adolescence are universal. What's your most mortifying teen memory?

4. Did you ever have a period of religious enthusiasm? What triggered it? What did you do?

5. Do you sometimes think you've been anointed for a special task? Share and discuss.

6. The Traigs have a fondness for impossibly tacky crafts. What's the tackiest thing you've ever crafted? Show and tell is encouraged.

7. Jennifer's sister Victoria has a history of messing with people's food. Have you ever contaminated someone else's meal? Share your answer after cake has been served.

Here Kitty Kitty

A novel by Jardine Libaire

"There are no easy epiphanies in this dark, tender book. Libaire instead wisely explores her heroine's long and difficult struggle to take care of herself: to be sober, to sleep peacefully, to be alone. In the process, the author offers glittering descriptions of New York life, both its obstacles and its promise."

— Suzy Hansen, *New York Times Book Review*

Oblivion

Stories by David Foster Wallace

"Stunning. . . . Wallace is an astonishing storyteller whose fiction reminds us why we learned to read in the first place."

— Andrew Ervin, *San Francisco Chronicle*

Gotham Tragic

A novel by Kurt Wenzel

"A cunningly written send-up of New York life that's both witty and unsettling." — Jackie Pray, *USA Today*

You Are Here
A Memoir of Arrival by Wesley Gibson

"*You Are Here* is a candid, revealing look at one person's life and obstacles. And although it can be dark and shifty at times, an undercurrent of comedy keeps it lighthearted and fresh. Baring his soul, Gibson makes this one of the best memoirs since Elizabeth Wurtzel's *Prozac Nation*."   — Nicholas Thomas, *USA Today*

Ballad of the Whiskey Robber
A True Story of Bank Heists, Ice Hockey, Transylvanian Pelt Smuggling, Moonlighting Detectives, and Broken Hearts
by Julian Rubinstein

"A madcap joy ride alongside one of the most endearing figures in the annals of bad behavior."   — *Men's Journal*

Dress Your Family in Corduroy and Denim
by David Sedaris

"Hilarious, elegant, and surprisingly moving tales of all too ordinary madness. . . . Sedaris is a complete master of the form."   — Chris Lehmann, *Washington Post Book World*